Dust in the Wind. . .

A Guide to American Ghost Towns

by Gary B. Speck

white's

Published by
White's Electronics, Inc.
Sweet Home, Oregon

Editor: Mary Hand

Acknowledgements

...To my wife Julie and our three sons - Jason, Jeremy, and Matthew, I especially want to say thank you for your patience in having every family vacation turned into a ghost town adventure.

...To my parents, for instilling your love of history and respect for the outdoors in my heart.

...To Rosemary Anderson, the editor of *Western & Eastern Treasures* magazine, for all your help and support over the past dozen years.

...To People's Publishing Company for permission to use previously published information from my monthly column *"Ghost Town USA"*, appearing in *Western & Eastern Treasures* magazine.

...To Mary Hand and White's Electronics for helping make my dream of writing a book come true.

...And last but not least, to the hundreds of fellow ghost towners who have sent information and corresponded with me over the past 25 years.

THANK YOU...THANK YOU...THANK YOU!

S COMPANY
18,000,000
SHARES
GOLDFIELD, NEVADA
Pay to
Yellow Aster Mining and
Pay to H. Wallace
TO THE NATIONAL
210693
EMPTY AT ONCE AND RETURN TO
S. O. Co.
LAWS, CAL.
54 NET GALLONS
RANDSBURG
YELLOW ASTER MINE
KELLY MINE
RED MOUNTAIN
Johannesburg

Ghost Towns

Those two words promise adventure to thousands of Americans who take to the highways and byways of this country in search of these lost or forgotten habitations.

Dust in the Wind –A GUIDE TO AMERICAN GHOST TOWNS will be their guidebook. Even so, this book is NOT intended to be an all inclusive guide to all the ghost towns in the country. Just listing the 30,000-50,000+ ghost towns and writing a brief synopsis of their history would take a book several feet thick!

However, this book IS a guide to some of the best ghost towns in the country. Although I have chosen as much variety as possible, there are many sites, especially in the East, where tangible remains may be a lot harder to find than in the West. I have also tried to span the spectrum of different types of towns ranging from socialistic communes to military posts, and from pre-Revolutionary War colonial settlements to twentieth century mining towns.

Many of the sites will be fee charging state or national historic landmarks or monuments, which may curtail the use of metal detectors. This does not diminish their historical value or worth to ghost towners.

I have not knowingly included any locations that

are closed to the public, either through land closures or being inundated by a reservoir or covered by a new freeway. Some may be a bit difficult to access, while others will be right off the Interstate.

Happy Ghost Towning . . . Bodie, CA

If you are fascinated by ghost towns, then this guidebook will lead you to many years of exploration and enjoyment. Let it be the key that awakens a passion to the wonderful world of ghost towns and ghost towning.

Happy Ghost Towning!

Gary B. Speck

Gary Speck

Dust in the Wind

Dust in the Wind. . .

Table of Contents

Dust in the Wind

Introduction

Curled wood battens peel away from the facade above a sagging, weathered canopy, standing only by virtue of a few rusty nails. Glassless windows stare blankly onto a rutted dirt street overgrown with native vegetation.

Glassless windows stare blankly onto a rutted dirt street . . . Keeler, CA

Dust in the Wind

Flaking paint of an unreadable advertisement is barely visible on the desiccated, chocolate colored wood wall. A tangled pile of twisted floor joists, rusty metal, tin shingles and who-knows-what-else is impounded by crumbling brick walls. A rusting bedframe leans against the storefront, and a faded gold "Visitors Wel..." decorates the broken remains of a front window.

Across the street, a solid brick building is fronted with heavy, wooden doors sagging pitifully on frozen hinges. Standing sentinel are two glass-globed gasoline pumps waiting patiently for customers who won't arrive. Mummified dispensing hoses lie twisted at the pump bases like a pair of dead snakes.

A slight breeze blows through open window casements and doorless entries, rustling the decaying debris of a dead town. The collapsing, empty building shells of the abandoned town are all that remain of the hopes and dreams of a community of people whose hopes and dreams have evaporated and blown away like dust in the wind.

Popular lore says ghost towns are only found in the West. Reality says "wrong!" All 50 states have ghost towns! Some historians estimate there are about 30,000 abandoned towns scattered across the country. I feel the total is closer to 50,000, or more!

That is a lot of ghost towns!

Most ghost towns with standing buildings are in the West because they lie on public owned land. Once the towns were abandoned there was no economic need to raze them. In the East and Midwest, most land is privately owned. Many times the owner of a property on which an abandoned town was located would demolish any usable buildings or at least render them uninhabitable. Why pay property taxes on an empty building?

So, what exactly is a ghost town?

Gary Speck

Webster's New Collegiate Dictionary defines a ghost town as "a once flourishing town wholly or nearly deserted usu. as a result of the exhaustion of some natural resource (as gold)."

My definition is a little broader. *"Ghost town: a town or community that at one time had a commercial or population center, and is either wholly abandoned or has faded greatly from its peak, and now is just a shadow of its former self."*

Ghost towns are America's least understood and appreciated historical treasures. Unfortunately the ones with tangible remains are disappearing far too rapidly. The majority of ghost town sites left in the United States are just that...barren sites, only discovered through research and lots of footwork. Others contain rubble, ruins, foundation outlines, collapsed buildings, and the general flotsam and jetsam of a vanished town. Remaining ghosts with standing buildings are commonly occupied by a few die-hard residents, may fall under federal, state or local protection, or are so remote as to be inaccessible to all but the most adventurous and physically fit hikers. With this comes a need to study them for what they are, tied in with all that the American Dream stood for—guts, glory, and gold! If you learn the history of the old town, it will come alive, breathing with the life of a time when a person's word was good, gold was easy, and life was simpler.

Over the past century, these brawling, bawdy frontier mining towns, raucous, rollicking logging camps and frenzied, fast-living railroad boom towns have been studied, visited and written about in hundreds of books and thousands of articles. From Maine's windswept coast, across the grainfields of America's Heartland and into the arid desert regions of the Southwest, American ghost towns are waiting to be discovered, explored and shared. Whether perched on a high mountain cliff, tucked into a forested valley, or squatting on a sun-baked desert playa, these rickety relics of Americana are rapidly becoming faded memories, and are as fragile and fleeting as *Dust in the Wind.*

The Western States

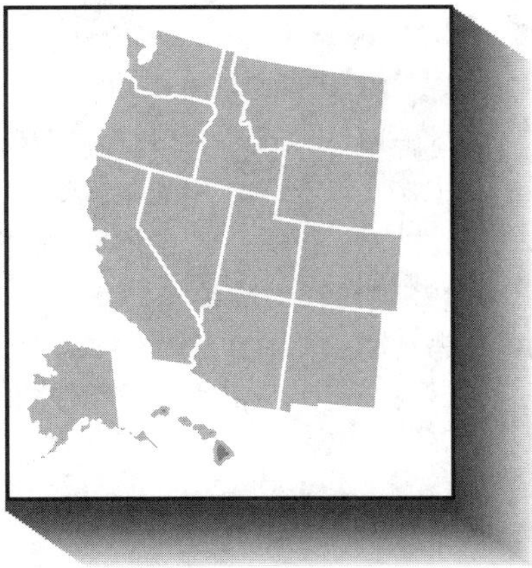

"This day some kind of mettle was found in the tail race that looks like goald, first discovered by James Martial, the Boss of the Mill."

It was on the cold, frosty morning of January 24, 1848 that James Marshall picked up the pea-sized gold nugget that changed California history...American history...and World history. The world's greatest treasure hunt, the California Gold Rush, was underway. Like tens of thousands of mythical Jasons, the argonauts came from all corners of the world... Europe, China, and South America, in search of their own golden fleece. Many found gold, and many were fleeced.

The hills were swallowed up and digested. Rivers rerouted, and their former beds scoured by the gold-crazed miners. And they found gold. Between the years 1848 and 1852, some $220,000,000 worth!

As the California Gold Rush faded, prospectors swarmed throughout the West finding gold, silver and other valuable minerals. Thousands of boomtowns popped up throughout the American West. Most of the towns were rooted in mining, but many were the result of farming, fishing, logging, and railroad building. Most have long since disappeared, many without even a trace, except a name on an old map.

From the Pacific shoreline to the eastern slope of the Rocky Mountains, and from the frigid reaches of Alaska's northwest coast, down to the balmy shores of Hawaii, are vestiges of these ephemeral communities. Many still exist as small towns, some quite lively, others nearly dead. Most are devoid of people, their sites littered with the scattered remains of buildings rapidly falling prey to the ravages of time, the elements and voracious vandals that have no sense of history.

The American West is where the best preserved ghost towns are located, and it is here we will start our journey.

Chapter One

Alaska

INDEPENDENCE MINE (Matanuska-Susitna Borough)
class C (SHP)-gold mining

On a gravel road northwest of Palmer.

A huge mill and over 25 buildings remain of this 1936-1942 gold mining camp. It was discovered in 1908 by Robert Hatcher, but it wasn't until 1936 that the camp boomed.

The camp consisted of the mill, bunkhouses and a mess hall for the mostly single miners, as well as a machine shop and aerial tram to haul ore to the mill. A visitor center and museum are on site to share the history of the mine.

NOME (Nome Borough)
class E-gold mining

On the underside of the Seward Peninsula, on the far northwest coast of Alaska.

In September 1898, the great Anvil Creek gold rush attracted up to 30,000 gold miners to the Nome area, forming a 15 mile long tent mining camp along the beach. In 1899 over $1 million in gold was panned, sluiced and washed from the beach sands.

Today, Nome is a frontier town reachable only by air. With a 1990 population of 2900, Nome isn't exactly a true ghost town, but in 1900 the official census showed 12,488 people in the town.

SKAGWAY (Haines Borough)
class E-mining supply center

At the north end of the Inside Passage, and Alaskan panhandle, at the mouth of the Skagway River.

During the great Klondike Gold Rush of 1896, Skagway was the starting point where the frenzied adventurers began their 500 mile overland journey to the booming goldfields in the Alaskan and Yukon interior. In three months it exploded from a single cabin to a boomtown of 15,000 people. Life here was a tough as the weather. It was a wideopen city offering to separate the Klondike boomers from their hard won money with women, booze or a card game.

Skagway held on as an outfitting center, and in 1990 it still had a population of about 800. Today, about 100 Victorian buildings remain in the largest and most often visited Alaskan mining town.

Other ghost towns in Alaska include...

CAPE YORK (Nome Borough)
class A-gold mining

100 miles northwest of Nome, this was another beach camp that boomed during the 1898-1900 rush.

EAGLE (SE Fairbanks Borough)
class Da-gold mining

At the north end of SH 5, on the south bank of the Yukon River, just inside the state line.

It acted as a fur trading center as well as a gold rush supply center during the late 1890's Alaska-Yukon Gold Rush.

THREE SAINTS BAY (Kodiak Island Borough)
class B-Russian trading post

On the southeast side of Kodiak Island. In 1784 the small settlement acted as the trading center for the Russian furring fleet. Around 1792 the town was destroyed by an earthquake and the resulting tsunami.

For the researcher...

FORTY-MILE (SE Fairbanks Borough...an old mining camp), IDITAROD (Yukon-Koyukuk Borough...1910-1922 gold boom town), KENNICOTT (Valdez-Cordova Borough...old mining town), TIN CITY (Nome Borough...at the tip of the Seward Peninsula northwest of Nome).

Hawaii

KALAUPAPA (Molokai Island)

class Da (NHP)-leper colony

On the north shore of the island at the base of the Makanalua Peninsula.

Kalaupapa is the remains of a large colony for people that had leprosy (now known as Hansen's Disease). It was founded in 1866 as a dumping place for those who got the disease. It wasn't until 1873 when Belgian priest Father Damien (Rev. Joseph Damien de Veuster) arrived, that the members of the colony received compassionate care. He almost single handedly served these people until he died of the disease in 1889.

Hansen's Disease is now controllable with drugs, so the colony is fading. Many of the longtime residents don't want to leave, even though in 1969 the quarantine restrictions placed on them were lifted. In 1991, the average age of the remaining 89 people was 68.

Other ghost towns in Hawaii include...

HALAWA (Molokai Island)
class B-taro farming

On eastern tip of the island, this busy taro farming town died in 1946 when a 36' tsunami wiped the old town off the map. A few ruins remain, along with a few newer homes.

KALAWAO (Molokai Island)
class B-leper colony

On the east side of the Makanalua Peninsula on Molokai Island's north shore, this was another 1866 leper colony, but it was established in a less protected location. By the early 1900s, most of the members had moved to Kalaupapa.

KEOMUKU (Lanai Island)
class C-sugar town

On SH 440, the east coastal road, 14 miles southeast of Lanai City. This tiny ghost town was a flourishing sugar town that died about 1901. In the 1970s there were still wooden buildings standing, one of which was a small church.

WAIPAHU CULTURAL GARDEN PARK (Oahu Island)
class F (reconstruction-$)- "sugar town"

In the city of Waipahu, below the Oahu Sugar Company Mill. This reconstruction of a typical sugar plantation worker's village is a living museum to the sugar era of 1852-1946. About 30 buildings representing various cultures, architectural styles and uses are located here. They were constructed from original blueprints, and are furnished with genuine period furniture and decorations.

For the researcher...

HOOPULOA (Hawaii Island...on the west coast of Hawaii Island), KEALAKOMO VILLAGE (Hawaii Island...heavily damaged by flowing lava from the February-March, 1971 volcanic eruption), RUSSIAN FORT (Kauai Island...an 1817 Russian outpost).

Dust in the Wind

Chapter Two

California

BODIE (Mono Co.)
class C/F (SHP/$)-gold mining

On SH 270, 13 miles east of US 395, at a point 6.5 miles south of Bridgeport. The last three miles are graded dirt.

Bodie, CA The ultimate ghost town!

To ghost towners, Bodie is the "Big One". Bodie is the ultimate ghost town, the best in the country. Over 150 structures have been "preserved" in a state of arrested deterioration. They are not gussied up, restored, or turned into a garish tourist trap, but preserved intact, as is.

In 1860, gold was found, and the resulting small mining camp grew slowly through the 1860s and early 1870s. In 1876 rich outcroppings of gold were found deep inside one of the mines. Word reached the outside world, and the population exploded. By 1881 Bodie boasted over 12,000 citizens.

Part of "downtown" Bodie, CA

Bodie's record for violence and assorted vices is legendary. Its wicked reputation was a source of pride for a town devoid of most of life's niceties and comforts. By the mid 1880s, the "Badman from Bodie" and a "man for breakfast" became history. The little girl whose prayer

"Goodbye God, I'm going to Bodie" created a newspaper feud, had moved on. Bodie slowly faded as the years rolled by. In 1932 fire destroyed 90% of the community, taking its will to live. When the government ordered the mines closed in 1942, Bodie rolled up its sidewalks and died.

Bodie State Historic Park was born in 1962, and remains as it did in 1962 when the state purchased the site.

COLOMA (El Dorado Co.)
class Db/F (SHP/$)-gold mining

On the South Fork of the American River, and on SH 49, seven miles northwest of Placerville.

On the cold frosty morning of January 24, 1848, James Marshall was checking the waterflow as he walked slowly along the tailrace of John Sutter's nearly completed sawmill on the American River. A glittering pea-sized rock caught his attention. He picked it up, and the rest is history.

The floodgates opened, and by the end of the year a constant stream of argonauts arrived in the region. Six months after the discovery, Coloma was a booming city of 10,000 people and a main street lined with hundreds of wooden buildings housing saloons, gambling halls, etc.

In 1850, when California became a state, and El Dorado County was formed, Coloma was named the county seat. During the mid-1850s, other rich gold discoveries throughout the Motherlode region sucked away the people, and Coloma shrivelled. In 1858 the county seat passed to Placerville, and a decade later only 200 citizens remained.

Today Coloma is a quiet town of 500 people, with many standing historic structures that date to the 1850s. California purchased most of the townsite in 1942, and today it is known as Marshall Gold Discovery State Historic Park.

LLANO DEL RIO (Los Angeles Co.)
class B-utopian commune

On SH 138, 20 miles east of Palmdale.

In 1913 Job Harriman, a political activist, and avowed socialist, purchased an old temperance colony site, and sold shares for a cooperative venture to prove to the world that true socialism could work.

Llano del Rio, CA

Shares were sold for a dollar each, and enough people purchased shares, so in October, 1913, the Llano del Rio Company was incorporated. By May of 1914, Llano del Rio's colonists began to build stone cabins with canvas tops, large barns and a beautiful rock pillared wooden hotel.

In 18 months, 500 people lived in the self sufficient

colony. However not all was rosy. Water supply problems affected crops, the state dogged Harriman, and friction in the community threatened the harmony of the colony.

By 1917 most colonists had left, and in 1918 Harriman lost Llano del Rio to bankruptcy. (See Newllano in Louisiana section of Chapter 15.)

The Utopian Socialism experiment failed, and today rock walls of a dozen structures, including the old hotel mark one of the most unique ghost towns in the country.

MANZANAR (Inyo Co.)
class B (SHL/NR/NHS)-relocation center

In Owens Valley, five miles south of Independence and on the west side of US 395.

Ruins at Manzanar, CA

A Japanese relocation center active between 1942 and 1945. It was one of ten in the Western United States built to house over 120,000 American citizens of Japanese ancestry, who were required to relocate from coastal regions and areas around defense plants to avoid "collaboration with the enemy."

Rows of wood frame barracks covered with tarpaper housed the 10,000 citizens. Central mess facilities fed them, and the camp had most of the amenities of a city, except it was enclosed by a barbed wire fence.

Gatehouse at Manzanar, CA

At the end of the war, Manzanar closed, and all the buildings except the two guard shacks were torn down. They remain as a mute testimony to the sacrifice those Americans were forced to make. Scattered concrete foundations and a cemetery remain.

RANDSBURG (Kern Co.)
class Db-gold mining

On the northeast end of the Rand Mountains, a mile west of US 395.

Randsburg is the best semi-ghost town in Southern California. It is a well-worn desert gold mining town of about 200 folks, most of whom either work at the Yellow Aster mine, try to cater to tourists, or are retired from life. Randsburg is not gussied up for tourists, and doesn't have the garish tourist traps that seem to inhabit so many historic old towns. It is a real, honest-to-goodness, desert mining town still clinging to life.

On April 25, 1895 three prospectors wandered over from Summit Dry Diggin's, a nearly forgotten old placer camp ten miles northeast. They found rich gold ore and soon the entire hillside was covered with mining claims. The Rand Mine paid the discoverers well. Despite a short period of legal entanglements, the camp grew, and in 1896 the Yellow Aster Mining Company was incorporated, the mine renamed, the 100 stamp mill ran around the clock, and life was good for the town's 1500 citizens.

Unlike many mining towns, the gold did not run out quickly. During the 1930s, 750 people still remained, and all seemed rosy until 1942 when the US Government ordered the mine to close. The Yellow Aster shut down after producing as much as $20,000,000. People drifted away, and by 1945, Randsburg was nearly deserted.

By 1990 the Yellow Aster Mine reopened, and today it is an active open pit mine fenced off to prevent trespass. Randsburg still has a few active businesses competing for attention with abandoned buildings.

Other ghost towns in California include...

CHINA CAMP (Marin Co.)
class C/F (SHP-$)-shrimp fishing

Chinese shrimp fishing camp on south shore of San Pablo Bay (northern part of San Francisco Bay). Northeast of San Rafael. Dates to early 1870s. In the 1880s had 500 people. Today it has a number of old buildings, and is a state historic park.

DARWIN (Inyo Co.)
class Da-silver mining

About 30 miles east of Owens Lake, and west of Death Valley, this old silver mining community still has a little kick, lots of old buildings, and a lot of atmosphere. It dates to the mid 1870s, and had several revivals.

GARLOCK (Kern Co.)
class C-ore milling

Garlock straddles Garlock Road, nine miles west of Randsburg. A few abandoned structures are protected by a fence, while others remain outside. The 1992 Landers earthquake heavily damaged the squat rock-walled saloon. Scattered about the desert scrub are the remains of other buildings that date back to the mid 1890s when Garlock was a booming desert milling town with several hundred people.

SHASTA (Shasta Co.)
class C/F(SHP)-gold mining

Brick ruins of this former gold mining city still line the sides of SH 299, 10 miles west of Redding in the northwest part of the state. It is a State Historic Landmark.

TUMCO (Imperial Co.)
class B-gold mining

Deep in the southeastern corner of the state, Tumco is 10 miles north of I-8. This gold mining camp dates back to the 1880s. After 1910 the mines were acquired by The United Mines Co., the camp boomed to a population of 2000. Today its roofless rock and adobe structures are still visitable, but a high clearance vehicle is required.

For the researcher...

BENTON (Mono Co...sleepy former silver mining town), HOLCOMB VALLEY (San Bernardino Co...old placer gold area with a half dozen ghosts), LUDLOW (San Bernardino Co...badly faded roadside community that has moved two times), MASONIC (Mono Co...gold mining camp accessible only with high clearance vehicles or four wheel drive), SWANSEA (Inyo Co...1860s smelting center).

Dust in the Wind

Gary Speck

Chapter Three

Idaho

BAY HORSE (Custer Co.)
class C-silver mining

Five miles west of SH 75 at a point seven miles south of Challis.

The silver-lead mines were discovered by Tim Cooper in 1877. A smelter and stamp mill were erected in 1880, and the boom began. In addition to the smelter, six charcoal kilns were built to supply fuel for ore processing. The main street was lined with wooden saloons, boarding houses, stores and other businesses.

In 1893 silver was demonetized and the economy took a tumble, taking Bay Horse with it. By the early 1920s, the town was deserted.

A number of wooden buildings are still standing.

GILMORE (Lemhi Co.)
class C-silver mining

West of SH 28, 18 miles south of Leadore.

Gold was discovered here in 1873, but it wasn't until 1889 when silver-lead ores were worked, the town actually began to have a life.

Because of its isolated location, a railroad was needed to ship the ore inexpensively, thus helping stimulate production in the mines and growth in the town. In 1910, the Gilmore and Pittsburgh Railway reached the struggling old town, and it boomed. The mines produced over $12,000,000 in silver and gold during the next 20 years. By the 1930s, the town died. Many buildings still remain.

IDAHO CITY (Boise Co.)
class Db-gold mining

On SH 21, 40 miles northeast of Boise.

Founded during the Boise Basin gold rush of 1863, Idaho City grew to be a city of 6000 people, and was considered for the territorial capital. An election was held, but it lost. After the election, Idaho City did not die. In 1865, only two years after the city was established, a major fire ripped it apart, destroying 80% of the buildings. The ashes were still warm as it rebuilt from locally produced brick.

After the boom ended in 1888, the town faded out, but always maintained some population. Idaho City has grown slightly from a population of 188 in 1960, to 320 in the 1990 census.

Today's Idaho City is an active small community proud of its mining heritage. Some of its standing buildings include the Catholic church, courthouse, Masonic Hall, newspaper building, territorial prison, and the Boise Basin Mining Museum (recent vintage).

SILVER CITY (Owyhee Co.)
class Da-silver mining

Located 21 miles southwest of Murphy, and 24 miles east of Jordan Valley, Oregon.

Silver City is the best ghost town in Idaho, and one of the best in the country. It was established in 1863 when the citizens of nearby Ruby relocated to a more hospitable location a mile upstream on Jordan Creek. The silver mines were exceptionally rich so the town grew rapidly. In 1867 Silver City was awarded the Owyhee County seat, which it held until 1935. Silver City's streets were lined with buildings and it is said that 20,000 people walked its now curled boardwalks.

In 1874 a telegraph line connected Silver City to Winnemucca, Nevada. Also the same year, The Idaho Avalanche newspaper was established.

By 1880 the boom fizzled, leaving less than 600 citizens. By 1942 when the government ordered the mines to close, Silver City was nearly a ghost town.

Today its handful of citizens jealously guard the remains of two dozen weathered wooden buildings and dusky rock walled structures, which include the Catholic church, Idaho Hotel, Masonic hall, a museum, school, and the Stoddard Mansion.

Other ghost towns in Idaho include...

BONANZA (Custer Co.)
class C-mining

Nine miles north of Sunbeam, which is on SH 75, 44 miles southwest of Challis. Bonanza was founded in 1876, and four years later boasted 1500 people and a busy main street lined with businesses. Some buildings still remain.

CUSTER (Custer Co.)
class C-gold mining

On north side of McKay Creek, two miles north of Bonanza, 34 miles southwest of Challis on dirt road. A museum in the old school house (operated by the Forest Service) and a few buildings are all that remain of this onetime gold camp. Custer was founded in 1876, shortly after General George A. Custer's defeat at the Little Bighorn River.

De LAMAR (Owyhee Co.)
class Da-silver mining

15 miles east of Jordan Valley, Oregon, and ten miles west of Silver City. An 1890s transportation and silver mining center, its main street stretched nearly two miles, along both sides of the gulch. $8 million in silver was dug from the local mines. Many buildings remain in the town named after mine owner Joseph R. De Lamar.

LEESBURG (Lemhi Co.)
class C-gold mining

On a four wheel drive road in the Salmon National Forest, 14 miles northeast of Cobalt, and 28 miles west of US 93 at a point five miles south of Salmon. This placer gold camp was founded in 1866, and quickly was home to 3000 folks, and over 100 businesses. A number of wooden buildings remain along what used to be the main street of this isolated community.

For the researcher...

BANNER (Boise Co...produced $3 million in silver), HELENA (Adams Co...an 1890s copper mining town.), MINERAL CITY (Washington Co...1880s town reached by four wheel drive road.), PEARL (Gem Co...a tough little mining camp), VIENNA (Blaine Co...rubbled site is hard to find).

Oregon

BOURNE (Baker Co.)
class C-mining
Seven miles north of Sumpter, along Cracker Creek.

Sumpter is on SH 7, 20 miles northwest of Salisbury.

In the 1870s, began as a placer camp full of saloons and other diversions, which lined a short main street. In March, 1895, a post office was established, and named after Jonathan Bourne, a mine promoter and US Senator from Oregon. At this time speculators took over when the mines faded out. The bubble burst, and Bourne faded.

The post office closed in May, 1927, and in 1937 the town was heavily damaged by a flash flood. Some mines are still producing, and a few buildings remain.

JACKSONVILLE (Jackson Co.)
class E-gold mining center

On SH 238, five miles west of Medford.

With a population of 1896, Jacksonville still has a lot of spunk. It is a colorful former mining town and center for a historic gold rush region. Jacksonville's roots date to December, 1851 and the overflow of miners from the California Gold Rush. As the original "49ers" spread out, many poked around in the southwestern corner of Oregon. They found gold, and dozens of small mining camps popped up in the forested wilderness of southwestern Oregon.

Today Jacksonville is a colorful collection of multi-hued brick and wood buildings housing an eclectic collection of small town businesses. The buildings were restored after World War II by the Southern Oregon Historical Society.

SHANIKO (Wasco Co.)
class Da-agriculture/transportation

On US 97, in north-central Oregon's high grasslands, 36 miles north of Madras, and 58 miles south of Biggs.

Shaniko began as a small sheep center in 1898, and by 1900 was the busiest wool shipping center in Oregon. It incorporated on February 9, 1901. At that time the town had a bank, a couple blacksmith shops, two story

Boardwalk to nowhere, Shaniko, OR

wooden city hall/fire station/jail, several hotels, two newspapers, a post office, saloons, school, two stores and many other structures. Church services were held in the school building.

A decade later, a new railroad routed through Bend pulled the traffic away from Shaniko, and it slowly faded.

By 1985 the downtown crossroad was still marked by the old two-story hotel, the town hall, livery stables and a strip of wooden buildings. A post office, general store and gas station still served the remaining 12 citizens.

Shaniko Hotel, Shaniko, OR

SUMPTER (Baker Co.)
class Da-gold mining

On SH 7, 20 miles west of Salisbury, which is nine miles south of Baker.

This gold mining town got its start in the 1860s

when three Carolinans settled and started farming. They called their homestead Fort Sumter, but when gold was found and the valley was overrun with Northern sympathizer miners, the name was changed to Sumpter.

At its peak in the 1890s, 3000-5000 folks live here, sharing space with 36 saloons along a long main street. The old town was wiped out in 1917 by a major fire, and has never recovered.

The Sumpter Valley Railway, a six mile long narrow gauge, was built to serve the area's forests, mines, ranches and homes. Today the restored railroad hauls tourists on summer weekends only. Sumpter has full services including four RV parks, a motel and a Bed & Breakfast inn, as well as a 1990 population of 150.

Other ghost towns in Oregon include...

AUBURN (Baker Co.)
class B-gold mining

About four miles west of US 30 at a point seven miles southeast of Baker. Accessible via four-wheel drive road. Only rubble remains where Henry Griffen discovered gold on October 23, 1861, and where by April, 1862, 6000 people made Auburn the largest town in the county. By 1868 Auburn was rapidly approaching ghost town status.

BOYD (Wasco Co.)
class Da-agricultural

Just east of US 197 about 12 miles south of The Dalles. This small agricultural community has faded from 150-200 people and a handful of different businesses. In 1985 all that remained were a few occupied homes, some abandoned ones and a grist mill.

GRANITE (Grant Co.)
class Da-gold mining

15 miles northwest of Sumpter, in the northeastern corner of the county. Originally located on July 4, 1862, it was named Independence. That name had to be changed because another Independence already existed in the state. The 1990 population of Granite was eight.

KERBY (Josephine Co.)
class Da-gold mining

Kerby was established around 1850, and through the 1850s was a major gold mining camp with some 500 people. It is on US 199, five miles south of Selma.

WHITNEY (Baker Co.)
class C-logging

A late 1890s/early 1900s logging camp and commercial center. Remains include a small handful of old buildings. Located just south of SH 7, 11 miles southwest of Sumpter.

For the researcher...

CORNUCOPIA (Baker Co...a wild town full of saloons and "sporting" ladies), HARDMAN (Morrow Co...agricultural ghost on Oregon's eastern grasslands.), MAYGER (Columbia Co... fishing village with spectral remains.), RICHMOND (Wheeler Co...another agricultural ghost in the northeastern grasslands.), VANPORT (Multnomah Co...a former company town.

Washington

HOME (Pierce Co.)
class C-commune

On east side of the peninsula on west side of Henderson Bay, 13 miles southwest of SH 16 at Purdy, which is 19 miles northwest of Tacoma. Several miles north of Lake Bay, and a half-mile from the "modern" community of Home.

Home was established in 1897 as a "freethinkers" colony. By 1900, 75 people called Home home, and the community had a reputation for uninhibited free love, and other "sinful" practices. Nudity and anarchist ways of life were tolerated, much to the dismay of Tacoma residents. Its mouthpiece newspaper was dedicated to the ideals of "Anarchist Communism".

Home was mostly ignored until 1904. After an avowed anarchist assassinated President McKinley they were looked upon as a threat, and the colony was shut down after a lot of pressure from Tacoma citizens.

A number of old buildings remain.

PORT BLAKELY (Kitsap Co.)
class B-lumber mill/shipping

14 miles south of Winslow on southeast part of Bainbridge Island, just north of Fort Ward. Across Puget Sound from downtown Seattle.

Port Blakely was a sawmill town founded in 1863. It had a huge sawmill that employed 1200 people, as well as a shipyard, blacksmith shop, large 2-story hotel, post office, several saloons and a school, all of which are long gone. A log pond was constructed by building a dam with flood gates across the end of the bay. When the tide came in the gates were opened, and the area flooded. At peak tide, the gates were closed, and at low tide the pond was still full.

For nearly 40 years the town prospered, but by the turn of the century, Port Blakely's boom days were over. Except for a minor resurgence during WWI, Port Blakely was history.

Remains include abandoned buildings and the rubble of wharves, railroad trestles and the mill. Along the highway a number of recent cabins and homes have been built.

PORT GAMBLE (Kitsap Co.)
class E-lumber

On SH 104, a mile northeast of the Hood Canal Toll Bridge, nine miles northwest of Kingston, 24 miles north of Bremerton.

A former company lumber milling community, which has been restored. Port Gamble was founded in 1853 by two men from Maine looking for a good place to establish a sawmill. In 1858 proper townsite was surveyed and laid out, and a town developed. In 1860, 200 people lived here.

A decade later, it had grown to 326 people, and the town consisted of the mill and warehouses as well as an Episcopal Church, grist mill, 2 large hotels, Masonic Hall, 40 student school, and many "neat and tasteful residences".

Many old buildings remain, some occupied, some not.

SKAMAKOWA (Wahkiakum Co.)
class Db-fishing

Skamakowa is along SH 4, eight miles northwest of Cathlamet in a shallow backwater along the north shore of the Columbia River.

This small, sleepy, former boomtown was a center for salmon fishing, canning and logging. It was founded in the mid 1800s when its only access was via riverboat.

That lasted until 1915 when the state finally constructed a road through the old community.

The town reached its zenith around 1910 when as many as 500 folks lived here. The town had a co-operative creamery, a huge wooden three-story hotel, meat market, saloons, a school, three shingle mills, a steam ship office, and other businesses along a quarter mile long line of wharf supported structures.

Today the shacks and historic structures are watched over by a handful of folks.

Other ghost towns in Washington include...

GOLD HILL (Okanogan Co.)
class B-mining

Near Loomis, which is 13 miles west of Ellisford. Ellisford is on US 97, 11 miles south of Oroville. The overgrown site is located on a four wheel drive trail.

KNAPPTON (Pacific Co.)
class Da-riverport

On the Columbia River and SH 401, several miles east of the Astoria Bridge. Originally established around 1870 as a cement plant, fishing and sawmill village, it was built on wharves extending out over the river. The sawmill burned in 1941, and the post office closed in 1943 thus ending Knappton's career as a viable community.

MARYHILL (Klickitat Co.)
class C ($ for museum)-agricultural

On north side of Columbia River, just west of the US 97 bridge that crosses from Biggs, Oregon, 18 miles east of The Dalles. The old town of Maryhill is rapidly falling to ruin, but the concrete reproduction of Stonehenge, and Sam Hill's house remain. His huge house is a museum that shares the history of this unique location.

NIGHTHAWK (Okanogan Co.)
class C-gold mining

Along the Silkameen River, 12 miles northwest of Oroville, and five miles south of the Canadian border.

A railroad reached the booming gold mining town in 1900, when it was at its peak. By the 1950s, the trains stopped, and the town faded. The tracks were pulled, and by the early 1970s all that remained open was a small general store. The rest of the buildings stood vacant, memories of the "good old days."

For the researcher...

COPPER CITY (Clark Co...gold and copper mining town), FRANKFORT (Pacific Co...fishing town located along the Columbia River.), RUBY (Okanogan Co...1890s silver town that has disappeared), VADER (Lewis Co...transportation center), WILKESON (Pierce Co...coal mining town).

Chapter Four

Nevada

AURORA (Mineral Co.)
class B-silver mining

East of the state line, about 25 miles southwest of Hawthorne, on a four wheel drive road.

Gold and silver were discovered in what became known as the Esmeralda Diggings in 1860. The next year Aurora was county seat of both Esmeralda County, Nevada Territory, AND Mono County, California! By 1864, Aurora had 10,000 people, 12 hotels, two newspapers, 21 saloons, 20 stores, and was found to be inside Nevada. Between 1869 and 1917 a few people remained, but it was deserted from 1917-1950 or so. The empty brick buildings made Aurora the best ghost town in the United States, but also a target for brick thieves since there was a huge demand for used brick. Aurora was reduced to a rubbled site in just a few years.

GOLDFIELD (Esmeralda Co.)
class Da-gold mining

On US 95, 27 miles south of Tonopah.

Gold was discovered in 1902, and by 1906 Goldfield was one of the trio of modern mining cities that popped up in central Nevada at the same time. With 20,000 people, a multi-block downtown core of three and four story concrete, brick, and cut stone buildings, electric streetlights, and a modern progressive attitude, Goldfield was building for the future as well as being the largest city in Nevada. It was a modern city of five banks, five newspapers (three of which were dailies), hundreds of saloons, and hundreds of other commercial buildings.

Goldfield Hotel, Goldfield, NV

Despite being ravaged by a flash flood in 1913, mine closings in 1918, and a 1923 fire that destroyed 53 square blocks, the spectral shell that remains is still home for a couple hundred people. The magnificent hulk of the Goldfield Hotel remains, as do a handful of unoccupied cut stone and masonry buildings north of the hotel.

Part of downtown Goldfield, NV

RHYOLITE (Nye Co.)

class C-silver mining

Three miles west of Beatty, and just east of Death Valley, CA.

In the summer of 1904 Shorty Harris (legendary Death Valley area prospector), and his partner Eddie Cross found some ugly green gold ore that assayed at $3,000 per ton.

A year later, this wonderful ghost town was a booming city of two and three story concrete buildings, electric lights, and 8,000 people. By 1907 that had increased to 16,000 and Rhyolite was at its zenith, joining Tonopah and Goldfield as one of the trio of Nevada's modern mining cities. Its amenities included bakeries, four banks, many hotels, three ice plants, law offices, two magazines, four newspapers, three railroads, scores of saloons, electric street lights, telephones, and anything else that could be imagined or needed.

A financial panic hit the nation in late 1907, which closed the door on mine investing. The city failed, and by 1910, only about 700 people remained. Some of the more substantial remains include the crumbling shell of the John S. Cook Bank, Porter Brothers store, the old bottle house, and the fenced off and occupied railroad depot.

TONOPAH (Nye Co.)

class E-silver mining

At the junction of US 95, and US 6, midway between Las Vegas and Reno in the heart of Nevada's desert.

Today's Tonopah of motels, restaurants, historical buildings and 3600 people is only a shadow of what it was in 1906, when it, along with Rhyolite and Goldfield, dominated mining in central Nevada.

Legend has it that on May 19, 1900, a down-on-his-luck prospector chucked a heavy rock at his burro, and that rock was rich silver ore. The source of the rock became the Mizpah Mine, which supported the mining town of Tonopah.

In 1906, the Nye County courthouse was completed and the county offices relocated from Belmont to Tonopah, which now consisted of five banks, hotels, an opera house, five newspapers, dozens of saloons, and the rest of the businesses needed to run a full-fledged mining city of 10,000 people. The Panic of 1907 didn't affect Tonopah too much, and from 1910-1914, the mines pumped out an average of $8.5 million per year.

In 1942, the government ordered closing of the mines did hurt the city. In 1947, the railroad was yanked, and things began to change. Because of its location on a major highway, Tonopah remained busy catering to passers-through. Today the clink of gaming chips and the merry ringing of slot machine bells can be heard coming from many of the 90 year old buildings that line US 95.

VIRGINIA CITY (Storey Co.)

class E-(touristy glitz) silver mining

On SH 341, southeast of Reno.

Virginia City started quietly enough in the early 1850s with some prospectors mining placer gold deposits. A thick blue metallic gunk gummed up their operations, and it wasn't until one of them had that gunk assayed that they realized what it was...$3000 per ton silver ore. Word reached the now depressed California gold region, and the call was "Ho for Washoe!"

A new town popped up on the east slope of Mount Davidson, and by 1863, Virginia City was a thriving city of 18,000 people. Through the 1860s and early 1870s, the mines produced well, and the town was very active.

The initial 1859-1860 rush and ensuing flush times were quiet compared to what happened later. In 1873, deep in the Consolidated Virginia Mine, super-rich silver ore was discovered. The price of Con-Virginia stock sky-rocketed, and Virginia City was THE place to be. It boomed to a population of 25,000, with 50 dry goods stores, 20 laundries, over 100 saloons, and hundreds of other businesses.

This lively semi-ghost of 920 people plays on its wild past. Alongside the garish tourist shops are the truly historic places. History is thick here, but it's overshadowed by touristy glitz. Virginia City is one of the best old mining towns to visit, ranking with Deadwood (SD) and Tomb-stone (AZ).

Other ghost towns in Nevada include...

AUSTIN (Lander Co.)
class E-silver mining

At the junction of US 50 and SH 305, in south part of county. This old silver mining town still clings to life with a couple hundred citizens and an eclectic collection of old buildings. It was the focus of the 1863 Reese River Rush that immediately followed the Washoe Rush of 1860.

BELMONT (Nye Co.)
class C-silver mining

An 1870s era silver mining town and former Nye County seat. Belmont lost those honors to the younger upstart of Tonopah in 1906. Here there are many crumbling reminders of a day when silver was king, and the town bustled with 10,000 miners. Today it sits on a graded dirt road 12 miles from Manhattan, and 46 miles north of Tonopah.

GOLD HILL (Storey Co.)
class Da-gold mining

Just south of Virginia City, and a suburb of that town, Gold Hill is the only other town remaining in the county. It was the location that the original gold miners worked during the 1850s, prior to the Washoe silver rush. It grew up with Virginia City, and had 8000 people by 1873.

For the researcher...

BULLFROG (Nye Co...a suburb of Rhyolite), DELAMAR (Lincoln Co...1890s gold town with 3000 people), SCHELLBOURNE (White Pine Co...started as a Pony Express station, then grew to a mining town of 300),

SODAVILLE (Mineral Co...early 1900s railroad town), TUSCARORA (Elko Co...an 1870s mining camp of 3000 people).

Utah

GRAFTON (Washington Co.)

class C-agricultural

On south side of the Virgin River, 3.7 miles west of Rockville, which is 35 miles east of St. George. Turn south off SH 9 onto Bridge Road, cross the bridge over the Virgin River and follow the graded dirt road to the right.

This old agricultural town dates back to 1859 when five Mormon families settled along the fertile Virgin River bottoms. The site was too close to the river, and in 1862 washed away.

The townsite was too good to abandon, so they re-settled a little further from the river. Within a couple years, several hundred acres were under cultivation with corn and wheat. Mulberry trees were planted and silk-worm raising became another industry.

In 1868, Grafton consisted of 28 families, and was at its peak. By 1900 only 120 remained, and in 1907 it was abandoned. The site has been used for filming of several movies, including parts of Butch Cassidy and the Sundance Kid.

Remaining buildings include the adobe brick school house, stucco covered two story house, a solid brick home, and a couple other buildings along with the remains of a several others. The cemetery is located 0.4 miles east of town, along the road from Rockville.

Grafton, UT. The bicycle scene in the movie Butch Cassidy & the Sundance Kid was filmed on this street

Don't forget your camera. The bright redrock cliffs to the north, deep green trees and unusually blue sky make this beautiful little ghost town one of the most photogenic ghosts in the country.

SEGO (Grand Co.)
class B-coal mining

At a point four miles north of Thompson a rough dirt road (passable only in high clearance vehicles) leads to the east, for a mile up Sego Canyon.

Around 1900, Harry Ballard discovered an outcropping of anthracite coal. Recognizing its value and potential, he purchased the land and began mining, eventually selling out to the American Fuel Company, who established a small company owned mining camp called Neslin.

In 1914, a railroad spur was pushed five miles up from the Denver & Rio Grande main line tracks at Thompson, to Neslin. The mines' profitability was low, so after a radical reorganization in 1916, the mining camp of 500 people was renamed for the Sego Lily which grew in profusion in the canyon.

In 1933 the miners were organized under the auspices of the United Mine Workers Union. The unionized mines continued to produce coal, but in 1947 the company sold the camp and mines to the miners, who formed the miner-owned Utah Grand Coal Co.

During the 1950s, diesel fuel replaced coal as the major fuel supply for the railroads, which reduced the need for coal. The mines shut down, and the town died. Many buildings were removed, flash floods washed others away, and trees and brush overgrew the former streets.

Most of Sego's buildings are now gone. Many foundations, collapsed dugouts, remains of cabins and an explosives bunker can be found hidden in brush along the creek. The solid pink rock walls remain of the old company store, and across the street is the deteriorating remains of what was once the two story wooden "American" boarding house. To the east, behind the store is the rock remains of another unidentified building.

Nearby ghosts include Cisco and Thompson.

SILVER REEF (Washington Co.)

class C/F (NR)-silver mining.

Located 1.5 miles west of Leeds, (EXIT 22), 15 miles north of St. George.

In 1866, silver bearing sandstone was discovered here, but the first claims weren't actually worked until 1874. Word got out and a rush ensued.

By 1877, the town had over 100 businesses

stretched out along a mile long main street. A race track, brewery and brass band were added attributes that many mining towns didn't have. In 1879, 2000 citizens were counted, but that year a major fire swept through town, silver prices dropped, labor disputes cropped up and water flooded the lower working levels in the mines.

By 1890, only 177 people remained, and in the early 1900s many of the remaining buildings were demolished. In 1908, fire destroyed almost all that remained. A few people remained behind, one of whom lived in the old dressed stone Wells Fargo & Co Express building until the late 1940s.

Restored Wells Fargo & Co building in Silver Reef, UT

Today, a number of summer cabins or "rural retreat" homes lie just north of the townsite. Silver Reef still has about 10 visible ruins, including the picturesque hulk of the Rice Bank Building. A museum is housed in the restored Wells Fargo building, which is listed on the National Register of Historic Places.

Other ghost towns in Utah include...

COVE FORT (Millard Co.)

class C/F (restored NR, SHS)-fort

Located a mile northeast of the I-70/I-15 junction, this is a restored 100' square stockade built to protect the local settlers. The army built it in 1867 and abandoned it in 1877. Private citizens then occupied it, and today it is operated by the Mormon Church as a historic site.

EUREKA (Juab Co.)

class E (NHD)-silver mining

On US 6, 20 miles west of I-15 at Santaquin, which is 15 miles north of Nephi.

Eureka is the metropolis of the Tintic Mining District, with a 1990 population of 562. It was born in 1869 with the discovery of silver, and sits in a shallow valley. The mines perch on the hills around it, and its false fronted-rock and brick building lined main street is now part of a National Historic District.

FRISCO (Beaver Co.)

class C-mining

On SH 21, 15 miles west of Milford. This old silver mining center's mines were discovered in 1875, and in 1876, the discoverers sold out and disappeared. Frisco grew rapidly, and claimed 23 saloons at its peak. The town also had a newspaper, the Frisco Times. In 1885 a major cave-in closed the Hornsilver Mine. This killed the town. By 1920, Frisco was completely deserted.

Inside the walls of Cove Fort, UT

MERCUR (Tooele Co.)
class C-gold mining

On a dirt road east of SH 73, about ten miles southeast of junction with SH 36, at a point 12 miles south of Tooele.

Mercur started as a wild placer gold camp of 1200 miners in the early 1860s, but quickly faded as the gold was exhausted. During the 1890s, hardrock mining began, and a second boom attracted 12,000 people. In 1902 fire destroyed the town. It rebuilt, but by 1942 Mercur was dead.

For the researcher...

ASAY TOWN (Garfield Co...abandoned agricultural community), CISCO (Grand Co...a colorful mural painted on an abandoned gas station), THOMPSON (Grand Co...ghost town with an AMTRACK station!), TOPAZ RELOCATION CENTER (Millard Co...WWII Japanese relocation center), and WAHSATCH (Summit Co...railroad boomtown three miles west of Evanston WY).

Dust in the Wind

Chapter Five

Colorado

CENTRAL CITY (Gilpin Co.)
class E-gold mining/milling

Two miles west of Black Hawk, which is on SH 118, ten miles north of Idaho Springs.

Central City with 335 people isn't a true ghost, but a small active community full of Colorado mining history. Since Colorado legalizing gambling here, plenty of tourists flock to see the "real" boomtown with its gaming glitz.

Beginning in the 1860s, Central City grew up in the early 1870s, and boomed through the 1880s, when it claimed between 10,000 and 30,000 people. It was considered the "richest square mile on earth", and contributed a large share of Gilpin County's reported $500 million + gold production.

CREEDE (Mineral Co.)
class E-silver mining

Located in the San Juan Mountains on SH 149, 22 miles northwest of South Fork, which is on US 160, midway between Alamosa and Pagosa Springs.

In May, 1890, the Holy Moses Mine was discovered, and the rush to Creede began. Flimsy wood shanties went up as fast as they could be built, and by the summer of 1892, 30 of them housed saloons. Others were made into boarding houses, hotels, restaurants, stores, and so forth, many of which were destroyed by a major fire in 1892.

The ore was rich enough so mining continued right through the silver panic of 1893, which killed many lesser silver towns.

It was a wild, isolated town with a population that may have reached 10,000. Some of the famed people that are said to have walked its streets included Poker Alice (a friend of Calamity Jane), Martha (Calamity Jane) Canary, Bob Ford (killed Jesse James), Frank James, Bat Masterson, and Soapy Smith(of Yukon gold rush fame).

Additional fires in 1895 and 1902 took out many wooden buildings, causing the citizenry to rebuild with brick and stone. If the fires weren't enough, floods washed through Creede's narrow streets in 1917 and 1936. Despite these calamities Creede survived, and it remains one of Colorado's many living ghost towns with a 1990 population of 362.

GEORGETOWN (Clear Creek Co.)

class E (NHL)-silver mining

Located just off I-70, at EXIT 228, about 40 miles west of Denver.

This is another of Colorado's mining towns that was too tough to die. A 1990 population of 891 keeps a watchful eye on this colorful mining town and its eclectic collection of 200 Victorian era buildings It is a living history museum untouched by the ravages of fire or flood, which preserves what is one of the best collections of late 1800s wooden mining camp architecture in the country.

In 1859 an accidental discovery of placer gold along the creek in this mountain rimmed valley attracted little attention. In 1864, a rich silver vein was discovered five miles to the northwest, and the site of the old placer camp suddenly swarmed with people.

Four years later the city of Georgetown was incorporated, and it wrested the county seat from Idaho Springs. It was the third largest city in Colorado with a population of 5000. In addition to the normal assortment of businesses, Georgetown sported TWO opera houses.

When the silver market crashed in 1892-1893, Georgetown crashed with it. It clung feebly to life, and in 1940 less than 200 people remained.

During the 1960s and early 1970s, disenchanted city folk rediscovered this gem, and a population resurgence began. Buildings were slowly purchased and spruced up. Now it is one of the most colorful, yet genuine of Colorado's still living old historic mining towns. The town attracts tourists, but avoids the hokey, glitzy, fake atmosphere that seems to prevail in Victorian-era mining towns.

ST. ELMO (Chaffee Co.)

class Da (NHD)-gold mining

This classic ghost is located at the west end of SH 162, 16.5 miles west of US 285 at Nathrop. The last 7.3 miles are graded dirt, and can be slick in bad weather.

The weathered wood buildings lining the main street of this 1880s gold town lie nestled in a beautiful high mountain valley. St. Elmo still has a few occupied cabins and an operating general store/post office, as well as a population of nine. The mocha brown, wooden buildings range from tumble-down shanties to a substantial two story hotel.

St. Elmo's gold mines were discovered in December, 1880, and by 1882 between 500 and 2000 people crowded into the small valley. The 1890s was the peak period for the town, whose businesses included dance halls, a

St. Elmo, CO schoolhouse

general store, five hotels, a newspaper *(St. Elmo Mountaineer),* post office, and saloons. A railroad even served the town.

A destructive fire in 1890 took out two blocks of businesses, and that part of town was not rebuilt. The remaining businesses were adequate to continue servicing the remaining 750 citizens.

In 1920, the Mary Murphy Mine shut down, crippling the town. Two years later the other mines followed suit, and in 1926 the trains stopped running. Today fifty or so buildings still mark one of America's finest ghost towns, the town of St. Elmo, Colorado.

Downtown St. Elmo, CO

Other ghost towns in Colorado include...

BOGGSVILLE (Bent Co.)
class C-cattle
Just off SH 101, three mile south of Las Animas.

Old jail and mining orecart in Silverton, CO

Dating back to the late 1800s, Boggsville was named after an earlier settler and friend of Kit Carson, Thomas Oliver Boggs. The town was damaged by a flood in 1921. Only a few badly weathered structures remain in this old town on the southern Colorado prairie.

EUREKA (San Juan Co.)
class C-gold mining

This old gold mining town is 8.5 miles northeast of Silverton on a rough dirt road (4-wheel drive only). The first mine was discovered in 1873, and it was so rich the isolated town grew rapidly to a population of 2000 people. It finally shut down in 1931, but a short revival occurred from 1937-1939.

SILVERTON (San Juan Co.)
class E-silver mining

"Apartments" in Silverton, CO

Situated in the heart of the San Juan Mountains, on US 550. 49 miles north of Durango.

This old community sits in a high mountain bowl at an elevation of 9300'. The many old buildings dating back to the 1880s make for a worthwhile stop. Silverton is also the northern terminus for the Durango-Silverton Narrow Gauge Railroad.

For the researcher...

ALPINE (ROMLEY and HANCOCK...Chaffee Co...small ghost towns in the high country above St. Elmo), CHEYENNE WELLS (Cheyenne Co...five miles north of present town), KEOTA (Weld Co...early 1900s prairie town), TABASCO (Las Animas Co...old coal mining town), WILLARD (Logan Co...badly faded prairie town).

Montana

BANNACK (Beaverhead Co.)

class C (SHM)-gold mining

About 35 miles west of Dillon.

Placer gold was discovered at "Grasshopper Diggins" in 1862, and word got out about the rich gravels of Montana's first big gold strike. A rush ensued.

After the placers exhausted themselves, hardrock mining took over, infusing the needed capital to make the town grow. From 1875-1881, 3000 folks lived here, and Bannack was both the county seat and territorial capital. The streets were lined with one and two story wooden structures as well as the two story brick courthouse.

Many weathered remnants remain in this, one of Montana's, and the country's finest ghosts.

ELKHORN (Jefferson Co.)

class C (SP)-gold mining

20 miles east of Boulder and due south of Helena.

Blank-eyed weathered wooden buildings stare across a weed-grown main street. Elkhorn looks like a Hollywood movie prop, but is a genuine, classic ghost town, another of the country's best. Like Bodie (CA), Elkhorn is preserved in a state of arrested deterioration. It has not been restored, but the wood preserved to prevent further decay.

The mines opened in 1872, but the real boom years were in the 1880s and 1890s. Elkhorn consisted of the normal compliment of businesses, including blacksmiths, churches, hotels, lodges, 14 saloons, stores and a railroad spur that delivered three trains a week. Between $14 and $32 million in gold & silver was extracted from the hardrock mines.

A few residents watch over this majestic ghost.

GRANITE (Granite Co.)

class C-silver mining

Several miles west of Phillipsburg.

Montana is rich is classic ghost towns, and Granite is another of these old towns full of chocolate colored, ragged wooden buildings that once housed saloons, general stores, hotels and several thousand people. Over $40 million in silver came from Granite's mines.

The original discovery was made on July 6, 1875, but it wasn't until 1880 that development of the mines began. In November, 1882 a major orebody was found deep in the Granite Mine, and the small camp exploded with people. By 1890, hotels, a newspaper, 18 saloons and other businesses operated out of a long line of clapboard structures.

The 1893 national silver panic shut down the mines, and the town nearly died. After a brief downtime, they slowly reopened, and Granite enjoyed a second boom from 1898-1904, when the mines produced about $1 million per year. In 1905 the mines shut down again, and the town finally died.

One of its most picturesque buildings was the three story stone and brick Miner's Union Hall built in 1890. On October 4, 1986, this magnificent building was burned by vandals, leaving only the blackened stubble of low walls.

Other ghost towns in Montana include...

BEARTOWN (Granite Co.)
class C-gold mining

Old gold mining town on US 10 near Drummond. The people here tried to obtain the state capital when it was established, but Beartown didn't obtain it.

GARNET (Granite Co.)
class C-gold mining

40 miles east of Missoula in the Garnet Mountains.

Garnet is another classic ghost town, this time preserved by the BLM. The gold was discovered in 1862, and the town sprouted almost instantly. It consisted of many wood and log structures and was active until 1912 when a major fire destroyed a major portion of the town.

MARYSVILLE (Lewis & Clark Co.)
class Da-gold mining

Gaunt wooden buildings and a few watchful citizens stand guard over this classic ghost. Dating to the 1880s, the wooden structures watched over $50 million in gold being pulled from the Drumlummon Mine (and others) and pass through the streets of this town of 3000 people.

RUBY (Madison Co.)

class Da-gold mining

Near Alder Gulch, Nevada City and Virginia City, Ruby was a small but busy gold camp that stood in the shadow of its richer neighbors.

VIRGINIA CITY (Madison Co.)

class Db/F (Touristy glitz)-silver mining

On SH 287, 14 miles west of Ennis.

Like its Nevada namesake, Virginia City is a gussied up tourist attraction. Despite the glitz, it still has much of its 1870s charm when it was Montana's 2nd territorial capital and home to 10,000 people.

For the researcher...

BLACKFOOT CITY (Powell Co...once had a population of 2000), HIGHLAND CITY (Silver Bow Co...once larger than Butte), MAIDEN (Fergus Co...in 1883 it had 150 buildings), PONY (Madison Co...in 1877, 1000 people lived here) and ZORTMAN (Phillips Co...in the Little Rockies.)

Wyoming

ATLANTIC CITY (Fremont Co.)

class Da-gold mining

Located 2.3 miles south of SH 28 at a point 23 miles south of Lander.

In 1868, gold was discovered here by prospectors from South Pass City. In a short time, 2000 folks populated this wooden boom town with four general stores, two hotels, an opera house, three restaurants, seven saloons, and the first brewery in Wyoming. A decade later the gold was gone, and Atlantic City was dead.

Today, a couple dozen well weathered buildings sprawl across a shallow slope overlooking Rock Creek. Tucked in among these buildings are a few modern summer cabins, and year-round homes for the handful of residents. Most of the remaining buildings are unoccupied, but a few are still in use, such as the Atlantic City Mercantile, and the historic old St. Andrew's Episcopal Church. Most of the town is posted no trespassing, but the older structures are near roads, and are highly visible.

PIEDMONT (Uinta Co.)

class C (private property)-railroad center

On graded dirt road 7.3 miles south of I-80 at EXIT 24

View to the west from the fence in Piedmont, WY

(Leroy Rd.), at a point 19 miles east of Evanston.

In 1869 Moses Byrne built five charcoal kilns near the small Union Pacific Railroad station of Byrne. It was going to be named after Byrne and his family, who settled in the region in the early 1860s, but to avoid conflict with Bryan Station just to the east, it was called Piedmont instead.

Piedmont rapidly became a wild camp full of saloons and gambling dens, which attracted soldiers from nearby Fort Bridger. Soon a general store, 2 story wooden hotel, newspaper, post office, and school were added to the collection of operating businesses, along with the Union Pacific Railroad repair facilities and roundhouse.

Old cabin at the fence line in Piedmont, WY

The Aspen Tunnel was built in 1901, and the railroad grade was relocated away from town. Piedmont's reason to exist died, and the town died. Today all

Looking east across the porch of the restored hotel in South Pass City, WY

that remains of this onetime boomtown are three restored charcoal kilns and the ruins of a fourth, all behind a gated fence. The town itself is just west of the kilns, and is just behind the fence of a working ranch. It is posted KEEP OUT, but the empty remains of about a dozen structures can be seen.

SOUTH PASS CITY (Fremont Co.)
class Da/F (restored...SHP)-gold mining

5 miles southwest of Atlantic City.

In 1866 gold was discovered in the South Pass of the Rockies by a group of former soldiers. Word leaked out about their find, and the ensuing gold rush added thousands of residents to the state, with some 4000 folks living in what became the county seat of Sweetwater County from 1868-1873. One of the more famous residents was claimed to be Calamity Jane.

South Pass City, WY

The half mile long main street was lined with one and two story commercial buildings housing such businesses as saloons, stores, saloons, restaurants, saloons, etc. By 1875 the population had fallen to 100, and South Pass City was a ghost town.

The most famous historical incident occurring here was a political tea held in the home of Esther Hobart Morris. Both candidates for the state legislature appeared, and they both promised that if elected they would make it legal for women to vote. Democrat William H. Bright kept his promise.

The east end of the town was purchased by the State of Wyoming in 1967, preserving the old town as a State Historic Park. It is free, although the museum will accept donations. About 25 buildings have been restored.

West of the restored part of town another dozen or so still occupied buildings serve the remaining populace.

Other ghost towns in Wyoming include...

BRYAN (Sweetwater Co.)

class B-railroad

On north side of I-80 along railroad tracks 12 miles west of Green River. Established in 1868 as a railroad center and repair shops for the union Pacific. It also acted as the railroad shipping point for the mines in the Atlantic City/South Pass City region. All that remains is the old cemetery.

ENCAMPMENT (Carbon Co.)

class E-copper mining

Copper was discovered in the mountains near here in 1898 and a 16 mile tramway brought ore to the smelter. A decade later the ore gave out, and the town faded. It is currently a center of tourism and agriculture located on SH 230, 10 miles south of a point on SH 130 71 miles west of Laramie. A museum and reconstructed complex of buildings share the history of the area.

FORT BRIDGER (Uinta Co.)

class C/F (Restored NHS, $)-military post

A reconstructed frontier army post located three miles southeast of I-80, at EXIT 34, in the town of Fort Bridger. In 1843, frontier explorer Jim Bridger established a trading post here. In 1854 the Mormons took over, and in 1857 the US Army obtained the site and built their fort. It was named for Bridger. In 1860 it was a stop on the Pony Express route, and was finally abandoned in 1878.

For the researcher...

EMPIRE (Goshen Co...early 1900s agricultural community), LAVOYE (Natrona Co...oilfield ghost that occupied two sites), MINER'S DELIGHT (Fremont Co...another ghost near South Pass City), OAKLEY (Lincoln Co...coal mining 1899-1942), and SHANNON (Natrona Co...oil company town from early 1900s).

Dust in the Wind

Chapter Six

Arizona

JEROME (Yavapai Co.)

class E (touristy)-copper mining

On SH 89A, 30 miles northeast of Prescott.

The first copper claims were filed in 1876 on the steep sides of Mingus Mountain. The Verde Mining District was founded, and by 1884, 400 people lived in the clapboard and tent shanty town clinging to the side of the mountain.

In 1886 copper prices plummeted, and the people left. Two years later, Montana mine developer William Clark purchased most of the operation, and by 1890, the United Verde was in full production and the town's population crept upward. Between 1897 and 1899 three major fires decimated the shanty town, and a new modern Jerome rebuilt of brick and concrete.

In 1900, 2861 people lived here, and huge structures such as the Montana hotel housed 1000 miners. The "Roaring Twenties" was Jerome's decade. During this period, the mine averaged $1 million a month. It all came to an end on October 29, 1929. The stock market crash sent copper prices plummeting, signalling the end of the wild times. In 1932, after producing nearly $1 billion in copper, the United Verde Mine closed, disrupting the lives of 15,000 people. Phelps Dodge Corp purchased the mines in 1935 and performed some exploratory work, and with WWII on the horizon with its demand for copper, the mines were reopened.

They closed again in 1950, and in 1952 the town could only muster 100 people. The city council grasping at straws proclaimed Jerome to be "America's Largest Ghost City". Tourists came, and by the 1970s the population increased.

Today Jerome has 403 people and an extremely active historical society that calls the town a "former mining community now on the road to restoration." Many historical old buildings and ruins remain, mixed in with arts and crafts shops and a few other businesses.

OATMAN (Mohave Co.)

class Da-gold mining

On old US 66, 20 miles west of Kingman.

In 1902, gold was discovered, but development was slow until 1908, when the Tom Reed Gold Mine hit a bonanza, as did the United Eastern Mine in 1913. A major boom swept through the ragtag mining camp of Vivian, giving it 10,000 people and a new name...Oatman.

Oatman was as wicked, wild and wide-open as they came. Isolated in the Black Mountains, it was a long way for law enforcement officials to go, and the town's folk knew it.

In the late 1930s, the Tom Reed shut down, and the town's pace slowed. Its location as the "Last Watering Hole" on Route 66, before entering California, prevented a sure death. Today, Oatman is a rickety relic of Americana with a couple hundred watchful residents who keep an eye on its main street full of colorful early 1900s buildings.

TOMBSTONE (Cochise Co.)

class E (touristy glitz)-silver mining

The "Town Too Tough To Die" is on US 80, about 75 miles southeast of Tucson.

This old silver mining community like Virginia City (NV), and Deadwood (SD) draws on a deep well of history, which is hidden behind a facade of hokey tourist-pulling glitz. In 1877 the Tombstone Mines were discovered, and by 1880, 15,000 people lived in this remote southeastern Arizona community.

Some of those folks included the Earp brothers. So much legend has been built up about them that the truth is difficult to ascertain. What is known is that brothers Wyatt, Virgil and Morgan were clannish, and they got on the bad side of the Clanton gang. Their famed street brawl and gunbattle has been immortalized as the "Gunfight at the OK Corral". Tombstone plays up that tidbit of Western history, and the tourists lap it up.

In real life, life was tough in frontier Arizona, and many men became legends whether they deserved it or not, and Tombstone's Earp clan filled the bill. *So be it.*

The Earps moved on, the boom days faded, and in 1929 the county seat was lost. To avoid becoming a ghost town, Tombstone relied on its fame to draw tourists. With old West movies and novels becoming popular, the old mining town found its draw capitalizing on the Earps, gunfights, and silver mines. By the mid 1960s, restoration of the town began, and today, Tombstone is a popular destination for tourists (especially non-Americans).

Despite its streets being lined with all kinds of glitzy gimmicks, Tombstone is a real honest-to-goodness old West mining town: a town whose true history and stories are hidden beneath the veneer of the tourist-drawing glitter.

Other ghost towns in Arizona include...

CHLORIDE CITY (Mohave Co.)
class Db-silver mining
21 miles north of Kingman and a mile east of US 93.

This old silver mining town dates back to the 1860s, but still has a little life left in it. Chloride City still has a half dozen open businesses serving the 300 or so remaining residents and a few tourists. It is the last surviving mining town in the Cerbat Hills, a town that in 1900 had 2000 people.

You can buy most anything here, and talk is free.
Chloride, AZ

CLEATOR (Yavapai Co.)
class Da-gold mining

Ten miles southwest of Cordes Junction, this old gold mining town still has a lot of buildings and a small handful of people to watch over them. It started life in 1864 as Turkey Creek, and didn't become Cleator until 1920 when it was a town of 1500 with over 60 buildings. The mines closed in the 1930s, the post office closed in 1954, and by 1960 only four people remained.

GOLDROAD (Mohave Co.)
class B-gold mining

North of Oatman, old US 66 winds through the heart of this old gold mining town. The gold was discovered in 1899, and a town soon built up in Sitgreaves Pass. By 1907 the mines fizzled, and the town shut down. In 1949 the property owner destroyed the usable buildings to save money on property taxes. Rock walls and rubble are all that remain.

HILLTOP (Cochise Co.)
class C-silver mining

On the east slope of the Chiricahua Mountains, five miles north of Paradise, this old silver mining town was founded in the 1880s. It remained a viable community until 1945. All that remains are a few buildings and ruins.

MOWRY (Santa Cruz Co.)
class C-silver mining

15 miles southeast of Patagonia, in the southeast corner of the county. An old silver/lead mining town that dates to 1857. In 1859, 300 men were at work here. It was active through 1907 when the mines were sold and shut down. Rubble, ruins and a couple buildings remain.

For the researcher...

CERBAT (Mohave Co...gold and silver mining town near Kingman), CROWN KING (Yavapai Co...in Arizona's "Motherlode" of ghost towns), HARQUA HALA (LaPaz Co...1888-1897 mining town), PEARCE (Cochise Co...peaked in early 1900s), WHITE HILLS (Mohave Co...now long gone).

New Mexico

CUERVO (Guadalupe Co.)

class Da-roadside community

Straddles I-40 at EXIT 291, 18 miles east of Santa Rosa and 41 miles west of Tucumcari.

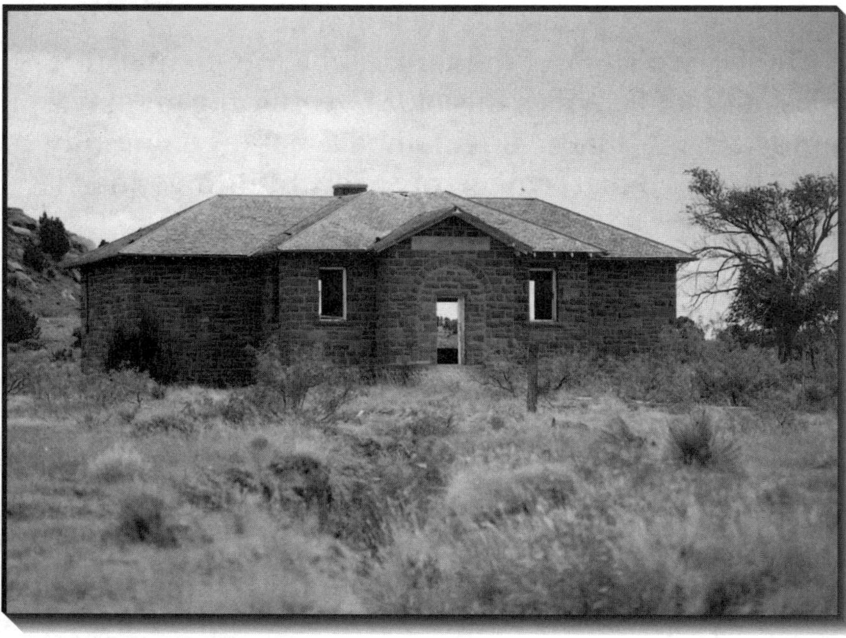

School's out forever in Cuervo, NM

With a population less than 100, and about 25-30 abandoned buildings mixed in with a dozen occupied structures, Cuervo is a ghost town worth visiting. The town was established around 1902, and was a major stopping point along old US 66. Today, the old highway is covered by I-40, which bisects the decrepid business district of mostly unused structures. Some of its more interesting buildings include the rock Catholic church, and 1930-1958 era school.

Adobe home in Cuervo, NM

GOLDEN (Santa Fe Co.)

class Da-gold mining

Located on SH 14, 38 miles northeast of Albuquerque.

In 1828 gold was discovered in the Ortiz Mountains to the north. Then in 1839, gold was discovered along Tuerto Creek. By 1845 the squalid adobe mining camp of Placer del Tuerto contained 100 homes, 22 businesses and about 250 people. San Francisco de Real was nearby.

American companies put some money into the mines, and the two small camps merged into one location called Golden. From 1887-1892, Golden peaked with the normal assortment of mining town related businesses. After 1910, Golden's aura tarnished and the town faded. A brief flurry of mining during the 1930s reawakened the town somewhat, but it has since faded into a peaceful slumber.

Downtown Golden, NM

Many ruins and abandoned buildings remain tossed haphazardly among the few occupied structures that comprise this sleepy community of 100 people.

LOS CERRILLOS (Santa Fe Co.)
class Da-mining

On SH 14, 25 miles southwest of Santa Fe.

Los Cerrillos began life in 1879 as a gold mining center

in the Cerrillos Hills. It is claimed the Spanish mined gold and turquoise here as early as 1582, but nothing of those days remains, including supporting documentation.

During the 1880s Los Cerrillos boasted a bakery, three hotels, a newspaper, 14 saloons and 2000 people. By the 1920s the gold was gone, but there was still some turquoise mining. During the 1930s-50s, the old town faded, and in 1958, Walt Disney Studios filmed several television series episodes here, and some of the buildings were restored for that. A few people remain, keeping a watchful eye on the remaining old buildings.

Main Street in Los Cerrillos, NM

SHAKESPEARE (Hidalgo Co.)

class Da-silver mining

Several miles south of Lordsburg.

This old silver mining town of the 1880s grew

rapidly and consisted of a population of several thousand. In 1882, the town was still small, and on its list of business ventures were an assay office, hotel, three saloons, and school. The 1893 silver panic killed the town, and in 1914 renewed activity created a rebirth that lasted until the mid 1930s. In 1935 the site was purchased as part of a ranch and the town still has many buildings and ruins remaining.

Other ghost towns in New Mexico include...

GAMERCO (McKinley Co.)
class Db-coal mining

An old coal mining town on US 666, three miles north of Gallup. Today all that remains of the old days is a tall smokestack, a coal tipple (headframelike structure), many mobile homes of dubious vintage and a few older cabins. the town was established in 1922, and named after the Gallup AMERican Coal COmpany.

KELLY (Socorro Co.)
class C-mining

Three miles south of Magdalena on the flank of the Magdalena Mountains. Kelly is an old mining town that dates from the 1870s through the early 1900s. At one time it had 3000 people, and the normal assortment of mining town businesses. Today many buildings remain in various conditions.

MONTOYA (Quay Co.)
class C-shipping center

North of I-40 at EXIT 311, 18 miles southwest of Tucumcari. Founded in 1902, Montoya consists of two crumbling brick and rock stores, a two story cut rock building that looks like it may have been a hotel, and a cluster of structures straddling the Southern Pacific Railroad. They include an old combination store/gas station and another roofless building advertising "Cold Beer".

This old saloon in Montoya, NM doesn't have "Cold Beer" anymore!

CHLORIDE (Sierra Co.)

class B-silver mining

2.3 miles south of Winston, the main street of this town is fronted by two story wood and stone buildings. The silver mines were originally worked in 1879, and by the mid 1880s, some 400 people lived here.

For the researcher...

CABEZON (Sandoval Co...many old buildings remain), FOLSOM (Union Co...1890s railroad town), MOGOLLON (Catron Co...one of the state's best ghost towns), ORGAN (Dona Ana Co...a number of structures remain), WHITE OAKS (Lincoln Co...an 1890s boomtown).

Dust in the Wind

The Heartland

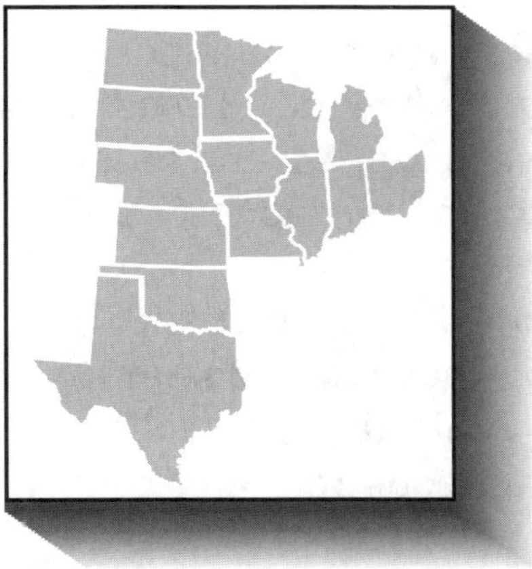

America's Heartland, the Midwestern states are not generally considered a hot spot for ghost towns, yet these 14 states contain thousands of old sites tucked in among the rolling hills and waving fields of grain. Other than South Dakota's Black Hills, this part of the country is generally ignored in ghost town literature.

The ghost towns of the Heartland vary from still living gold rush boom towns in South Dakota's Black Hills, to desiccated farm towns with a handful of people and a block long main street of unused, decaying brick commercial buildings.

Most of the ghost towns were agriculturally based. They have been created by the mass movement from rural to urban areas since WW II. Coupled with motor vehicles that drive longer distances comfortably and improved farm equipment that can work larger acreages, the need for many of these small towns has been eliminated.

Another aspect bemoaned by local residents is the

increased cost of doing business. Many wholesalers won't sell to the small Mom & Pop stores anymore, preferring to deal only with chain mega-stores. This leaves Mom & Pop scratching to find low cost suppliers so they can remain competitive and in business. With fewer residents the downtown cores of Mom & Pop stores have become unused, unneeded and unwanted. It's cheaper for shoppers to jump into the family chariot and drive over to the nearest large town and its Mega-Marts.

Another major source of ghost towns in the Heartland is relocation of towns. Many times a town would be established in a convenient location, but when the railroad came through, the town found itself being several miles from the tracks. It would relocate, and the old townsite would be abandoned.

There are other sources of ghosts in the Heartland, but those two factors mentioned above have caused more towns to die than anything else. Coal, silver and gold mining, riverboats, logging, the railroads, relocated county seats, and agrarian colonies have all contributed their towns. The Heartland is definitely fertile ghost towning country!

Chapter Seven

North Dakota

AMIDON (Slope Co.)
class Db-agricultural

Amidon straddles US 85, 35 miles south of I-94, almost directly south of Theodore Roosevelt National Park.

It was founded in 1910, and in 1911, the post office was established and named after district judge Charles F. Amidon. In 1915 Amidon incorporated as a village, and won an election to determine the county seat. The booming community had stores, banks, and newspapers, and now the county seat. In 1918 it re-incorporated as a city.

In 1930 the population peaked at 162, and began its downhill slide with the Depression. Amidon now has the dubious distinction of being the smallest county seat in the country. Most maps only show two towns in Slope County—Amidon with a population of 24, and Marmarth with a population of 144.

The county courthouse is a fairly recent, two story building sitting on well-manicured grounds. There is also an active "Country Store", an antique shop, library and school, senior center, and a number of homes, 50% of which appear abandoned.

BUCYRUS (Adams Co.)
class Da-agricultural

On the south side of US 12, 8.3 miles northwest of Hettinger.

Heartland skyscrapers, Bucyrus, ND

Bucyrus was established in 1907 by the railroad. It was first called Wolf Butte, then Dolan. Since there was already a town called Dolland in South Dakota, another name was chosen. According to Douglas Wick's book, North Dakota Place Names, a Bucyrus steam shovel was sitting nearby, and somebody suggested that name. In 1908 the Bucyrus post office opened its doors, and in 1930 the town reached its maximum population of 124. Today, the town of 22 people is a cluster of abandoned buildings. Only a church and half the homes are occupied.

No waiting here, Gascoyne, ND

CLEVELAND (Stutsman Co.)
class Db-agricultural

Just north of I-94 at EXIT 238, 25 miles west of Jamestown.

This small agricultural town was settled in 1882 by a group of folks from Cleveland, Ohio. The post office opened in the same year, but closed only two years later. In 1900 it reopened, and is still in operation.

On the west side of the main street are three vacant structures, a bank, grocery store, and two story town hall. The town hall had offices upstairs and a dance hall/ community center downstairs. On the east side of the main street, new modular buildings house the post office and town hall. There is also an older building that still operates as a bar.

Scattered about the townsite are grain elevators,

two newer churches, and the old school building with its newer appendage, the community center. Most of the homes still appear occupied, but as a town, Cleveland is fading.

On the south side of the railroad tracks a fairly recent combination store/gas station caters to the 121 townsfolk that remain in a town that polled 341 folks in 1920.

GASCOYNE (Bowman Co.)

class Da-agricultural

On the south side of US 12, 17 miles southeast of Bowman.

In 1907 the town was laid out along the Milwaukee Road railroad. The station was originally called Fischbein, but four months later renamed after one of the railroad's construction foreman.

The road to nowhere . . . Gascoyne, ND

In 1911, it was incorporated as a village, and reached its peak population of 97 in 1930. During its heyday, there were a number of active businesses including a bowling alley, the Cady Brothers' General Store, grain elevators, Gascoyne Lumber Yard, and a school. The post office closed in 1982. The lumber yard, grain elevators, bowling alley, school and two other commercial buildings are all vacant, along with the majority of the town's homes. Some of the homes appear to have been built within the last thirty years, and many of them are abandoned. According to the 1990 census, only 22 people still live here.

Other ghost towns in North Dakota include...

BURNSTAD (Logan Co.)
class Da-agricultural

On the DMV & W Railroad line just west of Beaver Lake, 42 miles south of I-94 at EXIT 208. Founded in 1906, the town had a post office from 1907 to 1979, a newspaper and other businesses. In 1930 there were 200 folks, but today only 20 people can be found here. Not much remains other than abandoned buildings and a few homes.

LEAL (Barnes Co.)
class Da-agricultural

On the SOO Line railroad tracks and SH 9, about 20 miles north of I-94 at EXIT 283. It was founded in 1892, and the post office opened its doors on December 28 of that year. Incorporated in 1911 as a village, it became a city in 1968. Its current population of 35 is much lower than the 1930 population peak of 105.

NOME (Barnes Co.)
class Da-agricultural

On SH 32, 19 miles south of I-94 at EXIT 302, which is ten miles east of Valley City. It has a population of 67. It was founded in 1900, incorporated as a village in 1907, and reached its peak population of 277 in 1940.

St. ANTHONY (Morton Co.)
class Db-agricultural

On SH 6, about 17 miles south of Mandan, this old community was first called Littleheart when it was laid out in 1890. In 1896, it was renamed by an enclave of Roman Catholic German/Hungarian settlers who established a large church and school. With a 1980 population of 75, down from its 1930 peak of 130, this small town is slowly fading towards ghosthood.

For the researcher...

APPAM (Williams Co...32 miles north of Williston), CRETE (Sargent Co...once had 200 people), GOOSE RIVER (Traill Co...onetime county seat), NOSODAK (Sioux Co...railroad construction camp), ZION (Towner Co...only a cemetery remains of this old Dunker Colony).

South Dakota

DEADWOOD (Lawrence Co.)
class E (touristy glitz)-gold mining

On US 85, 10 miles south of I-90 at EXIT 17, at a point seven miles east of Spearfish.

Deadwood ranks up there in Ghost Town annals with Virginia City (NV), and Tombstone (AZ). Deadwood is a historic old mining town with a 1990 population of 1830. It played host to the best and worst the Old West could offer.

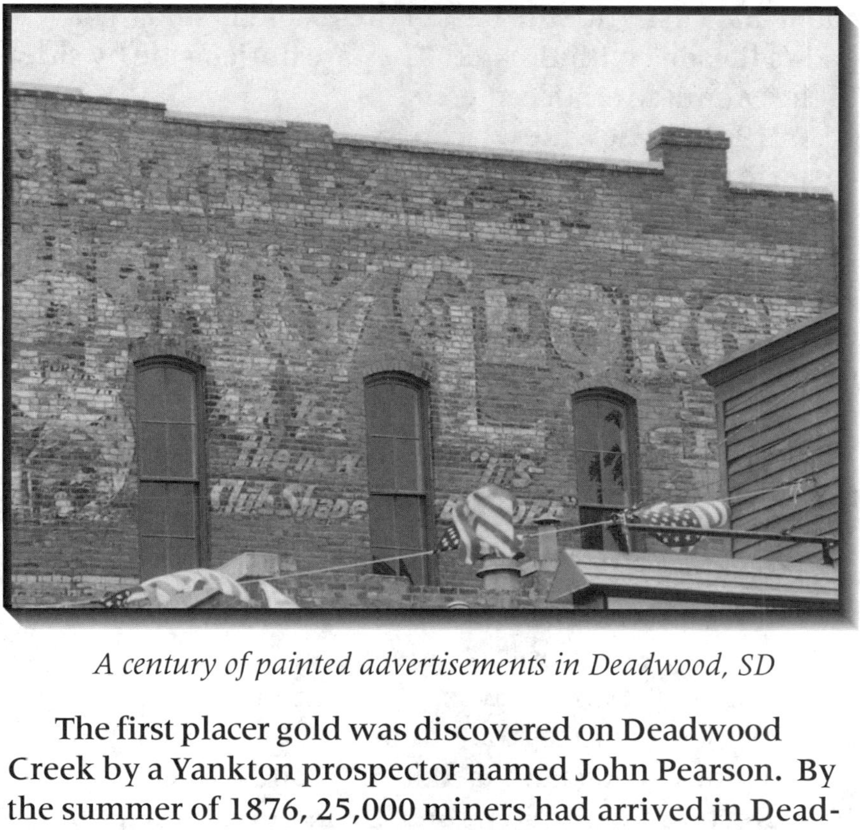

A century of painted advertisements in Deadwood, SD

The first placer gold was discovered on Deadwood Creek by a Yankton prospector named John Pearson. By the summer of 1876, 25,000 miners had arrived in Deadwood Gulch, and Deadwood City was booming. Fire swept through the city in 1879, and in 1883 a flood washed through the gulch taking out more of the town. The citizens banded together and rebuilt. Today the main streets are lined with 1-3 story brick buildings dating back to the glory days of the 1880s and 1890s after the baptism of fire and flood.

Due to its extreme isolation, the worst elements

of the West arrived, and Deadwood City rapidly grew into one of the wildest, wickedest mining towns in the West. Some of the more famous personalities that passed through include James Butler "Wild Bill" Hickok and Martha Jane "Calamity Jane" Canary. She could drink, shoot and cuss with the best of them, and is said to have had "a liaison" with Hickok. They are buried side by side in the Mount Moriah cemetery.

In 1961 the downtown core was declared a National Historic Landmark, and any new construction must match and blend in with the old. In 1989 gambling was legalized in Deadwood, and by 1991 over 80 locations offered gaming. Although gaming predominates the town's economy, the town looks more like an Old West boomtown than Las Vegas, due to a lack of glitter and neon.

Nearby, Lead is a still active mining town, and home of the fabulous Homestake Mine. Tours of the facilities are available ($).

ROCHFORD (Pennington Co.)

class Da-gold mining

On FR 231, 10 miles west of Merritt, which is on US 385, 20 miles southeast of Pluma.

Rochford was established in 1877 and named after M.D. Rochford, one of the three Deadwood hunters who accidentally discovered the rich gold bearing ore in 1875. By the end of 1878, Rochford had over 500 people.

A hundred years later, a number of wooden structures remained along with a small population and an operating store. The 1990 population was 50.

In 1995 there were two saloons, a fairly new community center, general store, mixed in with several closed business buildings and scattered cabins of all vintages.

Rochford, SD

St. ONGE (Lawrence Co.)
class Da-agricultural

On SH 34, 13 miles southeast of Belle Fourche, and six miles north of I-90 at EXIT 17.

It is claimed that this town was founded as early as the 1830s by the French. Today the small community of 100 has a decaying downtown core of unoccupied one and two story stone buildings sitting on a cross road. An abandoned school lies west of the railroad tracks, and a fairly modern gas station/convenience store sits along SH 34. There are a number of homes of various vintages from old clapboard shanties through recent mobile homes scattered about the townsite.

Part of downtown St. Onge, SD

Other ghost towns in South Dakota include...

CENTRAL CITY (Lawrence Co.)
class Db-gold mining

On US 14, midway between Lead and Deadwood, in the north end of the Black Hills. When it was established in January of 1877, it had a ready made population of 3000 miners. It eventually had four newspapers, along with the required saloons, schools, stores and other amenities for a city of 10,000.

Today 185 people populate this sleepy, non-touristy old gold mining town with its streetful of interesting old buildings.

MYSTIC (Pennington Co.)
class Da-gold mining

In the heart of the Black Hills, on FR 231, six miles

Blacksmith shop in Mystic, SD

southeast of Rochford. A once busy town whose remains in 1995 included the unoccupied assay office, blacksmith, chemical storage shed, granary, chapel and restored ice house which shared the site with two summer cabins. Along the railroad grade to the east, ruins and foundations of the lumber mill and yard are hidden by grass and brush.

PRAIRIE CITY (Perkins Co.)

class Da-agricultural

On SH 20, 17 miles west of Bison, and 37 miles east of Buffalo. This mouldering small town of 35 people has an old school converted into an antique shop, and the newer school appears used. There are also two churches, a closed general store, and an occupied combination post office/store/gas station, as well as a number of homes ranging in age from modern mobile homes to abandoned clapboard shanties.

REVA (Harding Co.)

class Da-agricultural

On SH 20, 23 miles east of Buffalo, this is another tiny Harding County town with a population of 10. It consists of a store/gas station combination with a warehouse and a mobile home rounding out the facilities.

For the researcher...

ALBEE (Grant Co...southeastern part of county), ASHTON (Spink Co...nice core of unoccupied buildings), HARDING (Harding Co...fading agricultural town), SORUM (Perkins Co...the railroad missed by 50 miles), and ZEONA (Perkins Co...maximum population was six).

Chapter Eight

Iowa

DEEP RIVER (Poweshiek Co.)
class Db-agricultural

On SH 85 eight miles east of Montezuma, and one mile west of junction with SH 21 at a point eight miles south of I-80.

This small agricultural town doesn't technically qualify as a ghost town using the criteria established in the introduction. BUT, the gaunt, block-long business district is lined with one and two story buildings that are 90% unoccupied.

There are also about 100 neat white clapboard homes, most still occupied, several churches, and at the east end a school and large cemetery serving the remaining 345 citizens.

GALESBURG (Jasper Co.)
class Db-agricultural

On CR T14, one mile south of the junction of CR T14 and CR F62, at a point 4.3 miles east of Reasoner, in the southeast part of the county.

One of the first settlers at the location was James Tool, in 1847. Others followed, including Laranzo Dow Earp and his family, who arrived from Monmouth, Warren County, Illinois in 1854.

Masonic Hall/store in Galesburg, IA

By 1855 the farmers needed a central supply and shipping location, so the town of Galesburg was established. It grew slowly, eventually consisting of four blacksmiths, a cemetery, four churches, three doctors, two general stores, a grist mill, harness shop, hotel, lawyer, Masonic & Eastern Star Hall, photographic gallery, post office, a school with 60 students, and a wagon repair shop. Most of the businesses were clustered around the town square.

During the Civil War, L.D. Earp's nephew Wyatt, came to live here for a short period while attending grade school. He later moved on to Pella with his family, and from there into infamy.

In the 1880s when the railroad pushed through the region, Galesburg tried to nab a station. It failed, and the town began to fade. Today all that remains are a park occupying the town square, the abandoned remains of the

Guernsey, IA's "Last Chance".

two story store, a stuccoed brick building, and a large barnlike structure that may have been a blacksmith. A church has been converted to a private home, and two fairly recent body shops round out the businesses. A number of homes lie outside the "downtown" cluster and most are lived in and well kept.

GUERNSEY (Poweshiek Co.)

class Da-agricultural

Half mile east of SH 21, and a mile south of I-80 at EXIT 201.

This tiny town of 70 people has a gravel main street lined with a dozen buildings. Only three, a church, the post office and "The Last Chance" actually look like they are still in use. Several others have been converted to homes. The hulking three-story brick school remains along the south side of the road.

Like so many farming communities in the Heartland, Guernsey began to fade after WW II, as population shifted to urban areas.

THORNBURG (Keokuk Co.)

class Da-agricultural

Located a mile east of SH 21, 17 miles south of I-80 at EXIT 201.

Downtown Thornburg, population 91, consists of five buildings, of which only the post office is operating. On the north side of the street are two unoccupied brick structures, and the tiny white-painted wooden post office. Across the street is the crumbling red clapboard Thornburg Grocery, and a combination brick/wood structure. Half the homes in this tiny town are abandoned. The only lively part of the whole town is the huge, modern, Tri-County School on the south side, and two active churches.

Thornburg grocery store, Thornburg, IA

TURNER (Jasper Co.)

class B-railroad shipping center

Five miles southwest of Grinnell, just south of Oakland Acres, and north of I-80 at EXIT 179.

It was founded as a Chicago, Rock Island & Pacific Railroad shipping center in the mid 1890s. A cattle stockyard was built in the 1890s. O.J. Turner opened a post office in his home on April 1, 1896, forming the nucleus for a budding town, which was platted in 1899. By the early 1900s, the town consisted of a blacksmith, cheese factory, coal yard, creamery, one or two general stores, grain elevator, ice house, lumber yard, pool hall (saloon), post office, and a railroad depot with a telegraph office. A grade school was located just west of town.

After a major fire, Turner faded rapidly during the 1920s, the post office closing on June 29, 1929.

Within several years the other businesses had closed, and the store was converted into a dance hall. By the late 1940s, the buildings were all gone, and in 1960 the last house burned.

Other ghost towns in Iowa include...

BENTONSPORT (Van Buren Co.)
class Db-steamboat riverport

In the far southeast corner of the state. With a population of 40, this tiny Des Moines River community focuses on its past. Coupled with the neighboring towns of Bonaparte and Keosauqua, they have consolidated into a major tourist draw called the "Villages of Van Buren."

FROELICH (Clayton Co.)
class Da/F (privately restored)-agricultural

Located on US 18, four miles east of Monona. This is a restored 1870s village that once contained a blacksmith, creamery, grocery store, post office, railroad depot, sawmill and school. It is also where the first John Deere tractor was built. The old town has been preserved by a private organization called the Froelich Foundation.

MOTOR MILL (Clayton Co.
class C (SHS, NR)-gristmill village

On the Turkey River, 6.5 miles southeast of Elkader. The restored seven story tall grist mill was built in 1869, and the rest of the community followed in the early 1870s. In the early 1880s the mill shut down. In 1983 the site was purchased from a dairy operation and all non-original buildings removed. The site is undergoing restoration to original condition. The mill and four buildings are done.

STONE CITY (Jones Co.)

class Db-limestone quarry town

About four miles northeast of Anamosa, this old quarry town along the Wapsipinicon River still has a half dozen structures built of locally quarried limestone. With a population of 50, it is a far cry from the days when it was a booming quarry town with 1000 people. Grant Wood (the painter of American Gothic) lived here and operated an art colony from 1932 to 1933.

For the researcher...

CALHOUN (Harrison Co...five miles north of Missouri Valley), HAUNTOWN (Clinton Co...near Clinton), LANGWORTHY (Jones Co...on US 151, four miles southwest of Monticello), MONTPELIER (Muscatine Co... original site of, and three miles east of present town of Montpelier), YOUNG'S MILL (Wayne Co...sawmill located on SH 2, east of Corydon)

Nebraska

ANTIOCH (Sheridan Co.)

class Da-potash mining

On SH 2, 15 miles east of Alliance.

Antioch is an anomaly among Nebraska ghost towns. It was a mining town. During the World War I years, potash was a valuable commodity for military use, and the area around Antioch supplied a huge amount of that strategic mineral. The small town's population boomed to over 2000 folks. When the war ended in 1919, and the demand for potash decreased, the people left almost as fast as they arrived.

By 1939, the population had dropped to only 147, and by 1980, only 25 people remained.

BURTON (Keya Paha Co.)
class Da-agricultural

Located on SH 12, eight miles east of US 183, at a point five miles north of Springview, 50 air miles east of Valentine.

In 1884, the post office was established, and a heated battle developed between Burton and nearby Springview to grab the honors of being the county seat. A year later, Springview was county seat, and Burton muddled along as a has been.

In 1940, some 104 folks still lived there. In 1973 the post office closed, and in 1990 the population dropped to nine.

ROCK CREEK PONY EXPRESS STATION
(Jefferson Co.)
class B/F (restored-SHP-$)-pony express station

About 6.5 miles southeast of Fairbury, in the southeast corner of the county.

In 1857, S.C. Glenn built a small cabin, lean-to store and barn to serve as a stage station and travel stop on the Oregon Trail. In 1859, Dave McCanles purchased the station, built a log cabin and excavated a well on the east side of Rock Creek. He built a toll bridge across the creek, joining the "West Ranch" and "East Ranch".

In 1860 he rented the East Ranch site to the Overland Stage Co. (parent company of the Pony Express). The station attendant was a company man, Horace Wellman.

In early 1861 a stable hand was needed, so James Butler (Wild Bill) Hickok was hired. Rather than renting the site, the Overland Company purchased the East Ranch from McCanles, and made a down payment, and the rest to be paid off in payments.

On July 12, 1861, Wellman went to Brownville to obtain the money, and he returned to East Ranch. Somehow, McCanles went to the station to get the money, and was shot dead by Hickok. The reason for the shooting is not known, but Hickok, Wellman, and stock tender D. Brink were tried for murder, and released after pleading self-defense. This is Hickok's first known fatal shooting.

By 1867 after changing hands, both the West and East Ranches of Rock Spring Station faded as traffic on the Oregon Trail was replaced by railroads.

In 1980 the state obtained the site and development and archaeologic exploration of the site began.

WINTER QUARTERS (Douglas Co.)

class A-temporary Mormon community

Just south of I-680 at EXIT 13. At 3215 State Street in north Omaha.

From 1846-1848 this was a camping place for the Mormons on their historic trek to what is now Utah. Monuments and replicas of a cabin are at the site, which has nothing remaining from the time when it was a temporary city of 3000 people and 600 buildings. A cemetery is one of the few tangible remains. It is the final resting place for some 600 travellers, but only a few graves are marked. Nearby is the Florence Mill, built in 1846 by the Mormons.

Other ghost towns in Nebraska include...

BAZILE MILLS Knox Co.)
class Da-agricultural

On SH 13, three miles north of Creighton. In 1882 the first woolen mill in the state was erected along the creek, a mile and a half north of town. Other woolen mills and grist mills followed, and the town became an important milling center. After the mills closed, the town faded, today containing only 34 people.

ELDORADO (Clay Co.)
class Da-agricultural

On SH 14, nine miles south of I-80, 25 air miles south-east of Grand Island. Only a few buildings remain from a town that once had 100 people.

No more school in Xenia, NE

STAFFORD (Holt Co.)
class C-agricultural

At the junction of US 20 and US 275, five miles southeast of Inman, this small community was platted in 1882. Its businesses included a Catholic church, grocery store, three hay barns and a hay office, post office, railroad depot, school and stockyards. All that remains are a weigh station and communication center.

XENIA (Sarpy Co.)
class C-agricultural

Seven miles southwest of Springfield, at the intersection of Buffalo Road and 192nd Street. On the northeast corner is the abandoned schoolhouse, and on the southwest corner the old store has been converted to a home. A half mile to the west is the cemetery.

For the researcher...

ANOKA (Boyd Co...post office open from 1902-1967), ENOLA (Madison Co...north of the city of Madison), KANOSHA (Cass Co...steamboat town near Plattsmouth), NEAPOLIS (Saunders Co...proposed state capital), SARPY CENTER (Sarpy Co...onetime booming wanna-be county seat).

Dust in the Wind

Chapter Nine

Kansas

APPLETON (Clark Co.)

class A-late 1880s boomtown

A mile southeast of Minneola, which is at the junction of US 54 and 283, 21 miles south of Dodge City.

During the 1885-1887 period, a number of heavily promoted boomtowns erupted across the face of southwestern Kansas. Only nine months after founding, this burgeoning community had a barber shop, two blacksmiths, six grocery/feed stores, two hotels, two meat markets, a weekly newspaper (the Appleton Era) and a restaurant.

The only thing missing was a railroad, and when that came through in 1887, a station called Minneola was established a mile northwest of the town. Today Minneola has over 700 people, and Appleton is a barren site.

ENGLEWOOD (Clark Co.)

class Da-agricultural

Located on US 283, three miles north of the state line, about 50 miles south of Dodge City.

Founded in 1884 this old town was touted as the "Veritable New Chicago of the Great Southwest." The Englewood Town Company promoted their new town and the people came. During the first boom from 1884-

1887, the town was platted, businesses went up and the future looked rosy.

Englewood was a wild, wide-open frontier town, drawing on the cattle herds heading north to Dodge City from Texas. It became an exciting place to live, and being so close to "No-Man's Land" (Oklahoma) helped.

1886 Englewood consisted of three drug stores, four dry goods/grocery stores, two hotels, two lumber yards, a newspaper (Clark County Chief), and a restaurant among many other businesses which probably included saloons. Englewood was "officially" a dry town, but due to its location and popularity, who knows what was served to the drovers?

Englewood, KS - closed for repairs!

By the early 1890s and the onslaught of depression and drought, many farmers went belly up, and their land was foreclosed on by various banks which also went under.

North side of the main street in Englewood, KS

This created havoc as parcel ownership became clouded. Growth was curtailed, and the town lost population rapidly.

In 1906, a rancher with clear ownership title to a parcel of land a mile and a half south of the old site offered his ranch as a site to replat the community, giving it a second chance. Englewood relocated, and this rebirth created waves of excitement in the faded old town. The new site slowly filled in, but in February, 1908 the entire west side of the business district burned to the ground.

That killed the spirit of Englewood's people. The town stagnated and began to fade, and in 1950 only 312 folks remained. By 1990, only 96 called Englewood "home".

Today the old downtown core east of US 283 looks like the stereotypical ghost town is supposed to. Its 100 foot wide main street is a two block long line of unoccupied buildings in all stages of repair from solid, to collapsing.

Other ghost towns sites in Kansas include...

BURDICK (Morris Co.)
class Db-cattle

A wide-open cowtown in the 1880s, Burdick today is located 60 miles southeast of Salina, and has a population of 70.

FREDERICK Rice Co.)
class Da-agricultural

On SH 4, 13 miles east of US 56 at Claflin, which is 15 miles northeast of Great Bend. Frederick has been beat to the ground by fire and tornados, and still maintains a small population of 18. It was founded in 1878, and by the early 1900s was a booming agricultural center. In 1934 fire destroyed most of the town, and it has never regained its vigor.

MINNEOLA (Franklin Co.)
class B-agricultural

Near Ottawa, south of Lawrence. (Do not confuse with the Minneola in Clark Co., mentioned above.)

In the 1870s, Minneola had a population in excess of 800. With a large business district, it was established for permanency. It was a serious contender for the territorial capital, but when Lawrence became territorial capital, Minneola faded, and today is almost totally lost.

SILVER CITY (Woodson Co.)
class B-mining

Near Yates Center, 50 miles north of Independence.

In the 1850s, what was thought to be silver was discovered. A rush to the location occurred. Buildings went up and mining shafts went down. When the ore was discovered to not be silver, the mines closed and the town folded.

For the researcher...

ALBANY HILL (Nemaha Co...former railroad town near Sabetha), CARNIERO (Ellsworth Co...1880s cattle town), HAMBURG (Pawnee Co...On US 56, northeast of Garfield), SANTA FE (Haskell Co...once had 1000 people), VESTA (Clark Co...1885 boomtown).

Missouri

SPLITLOG (McDonald Co.)
class A-mine promotion town

Here's one for all you researchers. The actual site is undetermined.

Splitlog was named after Mathias Splitlog, a Canadian Indian who founded the tiny town in the early 1800s. Not much happened until 1887 when mining promoters arrived and formed the Splitlog Silver Mining Co., and raved to the press how important their mines were. The railroad arrived, along with hundreds of people, but the scam burst, and soon Splitlog was a ghost town whose site is buried in oblivion.

WITTENBURG (Perry Co.)
class Da-riverport

Along the Mississippi River, 20 miles southeast of Perryville, and 75 miles south of St. Louis.

In 1839, a group of German immigrants founded this steamboat landing/riverport. It was ideally located along the Mississippi River and as the town grew, it also grew in importance as a transportation center.

When 1900 arrived, the bustling riverboat port had a population of over 700. The steamboats stopped running, the town shriveled, and in 1980 it contained only eight people, the smallest incorporated city in the state of Missouri.

Other ghost towns in Missouri include...

CHURCH HOLLOW (Cedar Co.)
class A-agricultural

In the southwest part of the state, 45 miles northwest of Springfield, Church Hollow dates to the Civil War, and consisted of a church, mill, several homes and a lost treasure legend worth repeating...

During the war, three men from a family placed their combined valuables in a large iron pot and buried it so soldiers or any other looters wouldn't find their valuables. It supposedly was never recovered.

DANVILLE (Montgomery Co.)
class Da-agricultural

On I-70, Exit 170, 43 miles east of Columbia. It was founded in the early 1800s, and was once the county seat. In 1864 Quantrill's Raiders (???) invaded the town, nearly killing it. By 1990 the town had faded to a population of 75.

(Old) FRANKLIN (Howard Co.)
class A-cattletown

On SH 5, north of the junction with US 40, near the present town of Franklin. It was a busy cattle town, and when the railroad was built, it missed the town by a couple miles, so the population moved to the newer site.

VAN HORN TAVERN (Boone Co.)
class A-roadside tavern

On US 40/I-70, five miles west of Columbia, this old roadside tavern site dates back to 1820, and is nothing but memories and a historical marker.

For the researcher...

CANE CREEK (Butler Co...small crossroads town with plenty of traveler's amenities.), FAR WEST (Caldwell Co...Mormon settlement with 4000 people), OZARK MILLS (Iron Co.), SANDY BRIDGE (Jefferson Co.), UMPIRE (Wright Co.).

Oklahoma

BOGGY DEPOT (Atoka Co.)
class B (State Park)-trading post/frontier town

15 miles west of Atoka and 2.5 miles north of "modern" Boggy Depot.

A trading post was established here as early as 1837, and in November of 1849 a post office opened. Within a year, Boggy Depot had become an important frontier town. Located at the junction of two important roads enhanced its position. It was also the capital of the Choctaw Nation, and during the Civil War was headquarters for a regiment of local Confederate soldiers.

After the war ended, the town remained an important location, but when the railroad passed through in the 1870s, it missed the town by a dozen miles. Boggy Depot relocated both to the railroad, and to a new site about three miles away. The old site quietly passed into oblivion.

It is currently a state park.

BRINKMAN (Greer Co.)
class C-agricultural

Nine miles north of Mangum and a mile west of US 283, in southwest corner of the state.

Established as a major railroad wheat shipping center in 1910. A post office was established along with a bank, hotel, restaurant, stores, and the ubiquitous grain elevators. During the 1920s the town boomed, and in 1925 the school had 450 students. The town had a bank, barber shop, cafes, two cotton gins, two grain elevators, hotel, and stores. It was quite active until the bank moved to Mangum in 1927, and a fire destroyed half of the business district in 1929.

In the early 1930s the state highway was realigned missing the town by a mile. Coupled with the depression and the Dust Bowl drought, Brinkman wallowed and faded.

The fifties were even crueler to the town. From a 1950 population of 150 the people continued leaving, and finally in 1965 the post office closed. By 1980, the population had dropped to only seven.

MEERS (Comanche Co.)
class C (NR)-gold mining

In the Wichita Mountains, 15 miles northwest of Lawton.

In 1896 gold was discovered in the Wichita Mountains, and the gold mining district boomed.

In 1902 a small town just north of the Wichita Forest Reserve was founded by miners, and it grew rapidly into an old fashioned gold boom camp. Doctors, a gold smelter, a grocery store, newspaper, post office and several other stores were established. It faded almost as fast when the gold was discovered to be shallow, and by 1905 Meers was dead.

The old restaurant/store is a veritable museum of Meers History and is on the National Register of Historic Places. The actual site of the old gold mining community is a half mile south of the store.

Other ghost towns in Oklahoma include...

KNOWLES (Beaver Co.)
class Da-agricultural

On US 64/270, 15 miles west of junction with US 283. An old agricultural town dating to 1906. In 1912, it relocated a half mile east to the railroad, and in 1913 reached its peak population of 254, and had over 30 businesses. The Depression and Dust Bowl killed the town. Today it shoulders the highway with the Knowles Country Store, a church, grain elevators, a cemetery, and 31 people.

LEHIGH (Coal Co.)

class Db-coal mining

On US 75, eight miles northwest of Atoka. Coal brought life to this location in 1880. As a result of the mines closing in nearby Savanna, the coal company brought 135 homes to Lehigh, and the population skyrocketed to 3000.

In 1907 it became county seat, but lost that honor a few years later. The town burned in 1912, and by 1980 only 287 people remained along with the abandoned downtown core.

OKAY (Wagoner Co.)

class B-frontier town

A mile south of "modern" Okay, northeast of Muskogee.

As Okay grew and prospered in the pre-Civil War years it had several names, six fires, and was occupied by the military during the war. It survived those calamities, but in 1871 when the railroad came through, the town packed its bags and relocated a mile to the north.

RICHARDS SPUR (Comanche Co.)

class Da-limestone mining

About eight miles north of Lawton and three miles north of I-44, this old limestone mining company town has many abandoned structures and a 1980 population of 50.

For the researcher...

CENTERVILLE (Kiowa Co...last buildings torn down between 1973 and 1976), DOAKSVILLE (Choctaw Co...pre-Civil War riverport on Red River), NEUTRAL CITY (Beaver Co...two miles west of Gate), SCULLYVILLE (LeFlore Co...1832-1865 when destroyed by Union troops), WIRT (Carter Co...early 1900's oil-boom town.)

Texas

BELKNAP (Young Co.)

class B-support town

10 miles NW of Graham.

Outside of and a half mile to the east of Fort Belknap, which was established in 1851. This was a goodtimes town that catered to the more prurient tastes of the soldiers.

By 1856 Belnap had 150 people, and became the county seat for Young Co. The town had a court house, hotel, post office, a saloon/pool hall, several stores, and in 1858 a Butterfield Overland Mail stage station.

In 1865 the county records were moved to Jonesboro out of fear of Union capture, and the town was nearly abandoned. The post office was discontinued in 1866. When the war ended, the fort was reactivated, and some prosperity returned to Belnap. By 1870 about 70 people lived here, but in 1872 the fort closed. The post office was re-established in 1874, but because of declining importance and population, the county seat officially switched to Graham. The town faded slowly, and in 1880 only 44 people remained.

In 1908, the post office finally closed, and most of the people moved to nearby Newcastle, leaving Belnap a ghost town. The fort was reconstructed in 1936, but the town remains only a memory. All that remains is its cemetery.

D'HANIS (Medina Co.)

class B-agricultural

1.5 miles from present town of D'Hanis

Established in 1847 by settlers from the Alsace

region of France. They built the St. Dominic Catholic Church of locally quarried limestone in 1853. It was used until 1914. A new church was built in 1913 and located 1.5 miles west of the old church. This served as the center for the new community which grew up around the church building. In 1893 a diptheria epidemic swept through the town.

PERICO (Dallam Co.)

class C-agricultural

On US 87, 24 miles northwest of Dalhart.

In 1888, the Fort Worth & Denver Railroad established a siding called Farwell. Nothing much happened until 1905 when the name changed. The siding consisted of a railroad station, the agent's home, and a few other people.

By the early 1930s, the town had become a farming center for that part of the county, and there was a farm implement dealer/store, gas station, grain elevator, lumberyard, post office, two-story school, and a large train station. As late as 1960 there were 40 people here, but by 1990 the town was dead.

TERLINGUA (Brewster Co.)

class C-mercury mining

Located above the Rio Grande west of Big Bend National Park, 80 miles south of Alpine.

This old mercury mining town began operations in the 1880s and boomed through the 1890s. In 1903 when the Chisos Mining Co. began to refract mercury from cinnabar ore the town and mines experienced a renewal. These mines produced a reported $40 million in mercury up to 1942, when the government ordered the mines closed.

During the peak years, the mine camp which grew up around the Chisos Mine was the largest of several in the

Terlingua District, with a population of 1000. It had company housing (simple adobe and rock hovels), a hotel, post office, store, and later on a gas station and movie theatre.

Many ruins of old buildings remain, and the site is famed as the annual location for the National Chili Cookoffs. The old store and a few residences have been re-occupied, and the 1990 population has increased to 25.

Other ghost towns in Texas include...

ACME (Hardeman Co.)
class C-gypsum mining

This old gypsum mining town was located on US 285, four miles northwest of Quanah. In 1890, James Sickler discovered the gypsum deposits, and established a milling plant. It was a company town, and in 1930 had 515 people. The town consisted of four stores, post office and a school. It died, and today the ruins of the old town are just outside the still active Georgia Pacific owned gypsum plant.

CLAIRMONT (Kent Co.)
class C-ranching center

On US 380, about 18 miles southwest of Jayton. It was founded in 1888, and in 1892, became the county seat. By 1900 it boasted 65 people, a post office, and had a two story courthouse with attached jail made from locally quarried stone. Through the 1930s and 1940s the population hovered around 200, but after WW II ended, the people left, and in 1954 the county seat was transferred to Jayton. Twenty people remain.

KELSEY (Upshur Co.)
class Da-Mormon colony

On Farm Road 1795, a mile south of SH 154, six

miles west of Gilmer. This small Mormon community was founded in 1898, laid out in 1902, and by 1917 had a population of 750, and 17 businesses. Through the 1930s the town foundered, and today is a scattered rural community, its downtown core abandoned.

SANCO (Coke Co.)

class C-cotton farming

On county road loop eight miles northwest of Robert Lee. The town moved in 1907 to its present site. In the early 1910s the town was at its peak, with a general store, two churches, a cotton gin and an automotive repair garage. In the late 1920s it began to fade, and in the early 1970s its last store closed.

For the researcher...

BRAVO (Hartley Co...shows on a 1938 road map, nothing today), CONLEN (Dallam Co...once had 150 people), FRY (Brown Co...oil boom town of 1920s and 30s), INDIANOLA (Calhoun Co...onetime huge seaport, destroyed by hurricane in 1886), SOASH (Howard Co...promotional town that never made it).

Chapter Ten

Michigan

COPPER HARBOR (Keweenaw Co.)
class Da-copper mining

At the northern tip of the Keweenaw Peninsula, on the northern side of the Upper Peninsula.

Copper was discovered here in 1843, and a small town developed. Because of its strategic location, Copper Harbor boomed as a copper mining, lumbering, and port town. It became the focal point of one of three major mining areas in the Upper Peninsula. By 1867 the mines faded, and Copper Harbor followed suit. Today it is a tiny resort, and a jumping off place for Isle Royale National Park.

A mile east of the site is Fort Wilkins State Park, the restored site of Fort Wilkins, an 1844-1870 Army post that was built to protect the area's copper miners.

FAYETTE (Delta Co.)
class C/F (SHP-$)-iron smelting

On small penninsula jutting from underside of Upper Penninsula, just east of Escanaba, just outside the present town of Fayette.

Fayette was an iron smelting center originally founded around 1865 by the Jackson Iron Co., and named after company manager Fayette Brown.

In 1892, after the forests were stripped of trees, the smelters shut down and the town of 500 people faded. It was never totally abandoned, and an attempted rebirth as a resort failed. In 1957 the Meade Paper Corporation traded it to the state of Michigan, and in 1959 it was designated a State Park.

Today the old community is undergoing restoration and consists of 22 cut limestone and clapboard structures.

PEQUAMING (Baraga Co.)

class Da-company town

On east side of Keweenaw Bay, seven miles north of L'Anse, on north side of the Upper Peninsula.

In 1878, the town was founded by the Hebard brothers as a lumber shipping center, and by 1883 it had 500 people, a church, general store, post office, school and a sawmill, all lit by electric lights. Henry Ford purchased Pequaming and over 400,000 acres of forest in 1922. He wanted to have control over the production of his vehicles by controlling the materials and their manufacture. The company operations employed some 1000 people.

The town was a company town filled with neat white houses and other niceties that were previously lacking in the rough and tumble lumbering world. Ford insisted on neatness, and lack of alcohol.

In 1943 the mill closed, and in 1944 the last school class graduated. Since wood was not used in automobile manufacturing anymore, the operation had to shut down. In 1952 new owners picked up the property and attempted to open it as a resort, but in 1968, they sold to another group of investors.

By the early 1970s a number of structures were razed, but many were spared, including the high school, caretaker's house, post office, water tower, warehouse and

Henry Ford's summer home (now a private lodge) among others.

In 1995 there were still 15 families living in the old town.

Other ghost towns in Michigan include...

EAGLE HARBOR (Keweenaw Co.)

class B-copper mining center

Located 15 miles west of Copper Harbor, this small mining center boomed from 1843 to 1867.

GREENWOOD (Marquette Co.)

class B-smelting center

Off US 41, just west of Ishpeming, this was an iron mining and smelting center that boomed between 1865 and 1875. It was a company town, supplying all the necessities for the smelter crews. When the hardwood forests were stripped, the smelters slowed, which affected mine production. When the smelters shut down the town died.

All that remains are a few ruins hidden in second growth forest.

HURON CITY (Huron Co.)

class C/F (museum-$)-lumbering

On SH 25, eight miles east of Port Austin, just east of the northern tip of the "heel" on the east side of Saginaw Bay. Huron City was a booming lumbering center destroyed by wildfires in 1871 and 1881. It was rebuilt several times, but when the town wells dried up, the mills moved on, and Huron City faded.

Today the site is owned by William Lyons Phelps Foundation, who operates the buildings as a museum.

(Old) VICTORIA (Ontanagon Co.)

class C (partially restored)-copper mining

Four miles southwest of Rockland. Victoria was a company copper mining town founded in 1847. It reached a population of 1800, many of whom were Cornish miners. The mines were active until 1921.

For the researcher...

BEAVER ISLAND (Charlevoix Co...French and Mormon colonies), DRUMMOND ISLAND (Chippewa Co...logging camps and lumber mills), QUINCY MINE (Houghton Co...copper mine active through 1945), SINGAPORE (Allegan Co...1860s lumber town), YANKEE SPRINGS (1830s stage station and tavern).

Minnesota

LOTHROP (Cass Co.)

class A-logging

Near Hackensack, which is on SH 371, south of Bemidji.

In the last half of the 1800s, this booming logging and railroad town was the end of the track for the lumbering companies. At its peak, the town consisted of 2000 people, two bakers, two barbers, a butcher, drug store, three grocery stores, two hotels, three or four restaurants, and a couple saloons. It was a typical hell-raising, end of tracks town. A train load of logs on their way to Brainerd passed through town every 20 minutes or so. There they were dumped into the Mississippi River and floated downstream to mills.

In 1896, the railroad was extended deeper into the woods, and Lothrop began to fade, as trade shifted to a new "end-of-the-track". In 1904, the depot building was moved to nearby Hackensack, and that town began to boom at Lothrop's expense.

WASIOJA (Dodge Co.)
class Db-agricultural

On CR 16, six miles northwest of Mantorville.

This small agricultural town of 80 people has about 50% of its buildings unoccupied. The weathered two story, wood frame and stone school building is one of them. Just to the northeast of it is the bright white, single story, clapboard, New England style Wasioja town hall. It was originally the First Baptist Church, and was erected in 1858.

Old schoolhouse, Wasioja, MN

The third building of historic value is a small squat limestone building that sits in the southwest corner of town. The structure was originally built in 1855 and used as a law office for Colonel George, and a bank building as well as the town's meeting center. In April, 1861, the building was converted for use as a recruiting station to enlist troops for the Civil War. This small station signed up over 200 men, and is the only remaining recruiting station left in the state of Minnesota.

Reconstructed Civil War recruiting station, Wasioja, MN

After the Civil War was over, the building subsequently served as a jail, office, storehouse, and private residence. In the 1960s, it was purchased by the Dodge County Historical Society, and in 1987 restoration began. That project was completed in July, 1988.

Other ghost towns in Minnesota include...

FORESTVILLE (Fillmore Co.)
class C/F (restored)-logging

A restored logging town with guides showing what life was like in a typical 1800's logging town. In early June there is an annual festival at the restored community. Forestville was active between 1855 and 1868, and had about 200 residents, a company store, school and workers' cabins. It is south of SH 16, six miles west of Preston.

GRAND PORTAGE (Cook Co.)
class C/F (restored-NM)-trading post

On the far northeastern tip of the state, this National Monument is a partially restored 18th Century North-West Company fur trading post. It was occupied from 1784-1803. It was originally established in 1731 by LaVerendrye.

OWATONNA PRISONER OF WAR CAMP (Steele Co.)
class B-WW II German POW camp

On the north edge of Owatonna, just off I-35. This prisoner of war camp began in April, 1944. At any one time there were between 50 and 273 prisoners. They worked in nearby farm fields or at the Owatonna Canning Co. plant, and lived in tents and clapboard barracks. In 1986, the mess hall was still standing and the site was still marked by numerous foundations.

SWIFT (Roseau Co.)
class Da-backwoods town

On SH 11, five miles southeast of Warroad, just south of the west end of Lake of the Woods. With a 1990 population of only 30, this tiny town is nearly a ghost. There were a number of commercial buildings here at one time, including a hotel.

For the researcher...

FRONTENAC (Goodhue Co...along the Mississippi River.), HANLEY FALLS (Yellow Medicine Co...original site one mile west of present site), LONDON (Cook Co...reachable only by horseback or four wheel drive), SACRAMENTO (Dodge Co...small 1855 gold camp near Rochester.)

Wisconsin

APOSTLE ISLANDS (Ashland and Bayfield Cos.)
class B/E-resort/early settlement

These islands are located off the northern tip of the state, about three miles east of Bayfield.

The earliest known settlement was a French fur trading post established in 1693. In 1793 the English established a trading post on Madeline Island, and in 1816, the American Fur Co established their headquarters in La Pointe.

During the mid 1800s the islands were logged heavily, quarried for the heavy "brownstone" sandstone, and were regional centers for fishing and furring. By the end of the 19th century, and early part of the 20th, many summer homes and resorts had been established.

Since 1970, the islands have been protected as a National Lakeshore, and second growth timber has virtually restored the islands to their former glory. By 1990, only Madeline Island was still occupied, all 147 people lived in the tiny town of La Pointe.

(Old) BELMONT (LaFayette Co.)

class C (restored)-capital city

On CR G, three miles northwest of the present town of Belmont.

Founded in 1836, Belmont served as the first capital of Wisconsin Territory. The territorial legislature disliked the location, and felt a more central spot would better serve their constituants. They met in a two story wood frame structure, and after 46 days voted to move the capitol to the upstart little community of Madison.

Shortly after the capital was moved, the railroad and the town were relocated three miles away, and old Belmont was an abandoned shell.

The old territorial capitol and Supreme Court buildings have been restored and are open as a museum and a state park.

COOKSVILLE (Rock Co.)

class Db-agriculture

Midway between Madison and Janesville, in northwest corner of county at junction of SH 59 and SH 138.

In 1842 the village was founded and named after John Cook. Homes and businesses were built, and the community grew. Unfortunately, when the railroad passed through the region, the town was bypassed, and it began to fade.

With a 1990 population of 80, and over 50 buildings on the National Register, this tiny hamlet is a worthwhile stop. The old fashioned general store is still open, and as of 1995, the town still had an active blacksmith.

PENDARVIS (Iowa Co.)

class C/F (restored-$)-lead mining

Located on US 151 near Mineral Point, 48 miles southwest of Madison.

From its founding in 1827 through the mass

exodus for the California gold fields in 1848-50, Mineral Point was a booming, rough-and-ready lead mining camp, full of Cornish miners. Today this active community has 2500 people, and is full of historic structures.

Nearby is Pendarvis. This was a small Cornish community of 30 or so buildings. The Cornish miners came from the Cornwall region of England, and spread out throughout the mining regions of the United States. Here they built limestone cottages and engaged in lead mining.

After the miners left, the abandoned buildings were torn down as they fell into ruin. In 1935 one of the homes was restored, and others followed suit. Today this cluster of six carefully restored rock and timber buildings is one of the Historical Society of Wisconsin's designated historic sites.

St. FERIOLE ISLAND (Crawford Co.)

class C-pioneer townsite

Along the east side of the Mississippi River, just west of downtown Prairie du Chien, near the confluence of the Mississippi and the Wisconsin Rivers.

An interesting collection of scattered buildings remain in this, the oldest area of Prairie du Chien. The island was the original site of the town, but due to continued flooding by the Mississippi River, the buildings were condemned by the Army Corps of Engineers, and hundreds were either demolished or removed. A dozen buildings of different types remain, and some are undergoing restoration.

The site dates back to at least 1673 when the French established a fur trading center on the island. During the period from 1685-1831, there were also four different military posts established by the governments of France, England and USA.

Around 1812, a huge stone warehouse was built by the American Fur Company to store their furs for shipping. It

Old warehouse on St. Feriole Island, WI

is still standing. Hercules Louis Dousman arrived in 1826, and as an agent for the American Fur Company, began to develop the site. In 1870 he built the oppulent mansion now known as the Villa Louis ($).

Other ghost towns in Wisconsin include...

BLUFF SIDING (Buffalo Co.)
class B-railroad

Located on the east bank of the Mississippi River across the river from Winona, MN., at the junction of SH 35 with CR M, in southern tip of county. This is an old railroad station that once had a hotel, two saloons, and a store as well as a lime kiln. Not much remains.

CREAM (Buffalo Co.)

class Da-agricultural

On SH 88, at the junction with CR E, east of Alma. At its peak, the small community consisted of a blacksmith shop, general store, hotel, post office, two saloons, and a school. Settled by German farmers, the town was a busy spot during the Prohibition era. 1990 population was only 30.

KNOWLETON (Marathon Co.)

class Da-logging

A busy 1800s logging town that has almost disappeared. In 1990 it was a store and gas station along with 80 people. It is located on US 51, 16 miles south of Wausau.

SUGAR BUSH & WILLIAMSONVILLE (Marinette Co.)

class A-lumbering.

Both of these towns were leveled in the great 1.28 million acre wildfire that raced through northeast Wisconsin and the southeast end of Michigan's Upper Peninsula on October 8, 1871. This fire is claimed to have killed between 1100 and 1500 people, and was the worst fire, in the terms of lives lost, in US history. Both towns lost about 200 people. The great Chicago Fire occured the same day!

For the researcher...

CONOVER (Vilas Co...one-time logging center), EMERSON (Iron Co...onetime lumbermill town), GORDON CITY (Burnett Co...1855-1868 milling town), HELENA (Iowa Co...former Wisconsin River port), NESHONOC (LaCrosse Co...town moved and changed name to West Salem in 1858).

Chapter Eleven

Illinois

BISHOP HILL (Henry Co.)

class C/F (restored-SHS)-religious colony

Two miles northwest of the present town of Bishop Hill, southwest of Kewanee.

Erik Janson, the leader of a Swedish dissident group founded this religious colony in 1846. The colony was named for Janson's birthplace, Biskopskula, Sweden. Ideologically the colony was a communistic utopia, with a religious bent. They believed the way to salvation was through simplicity. As the Civil War raged to the south, dissention in the commune caused it to fail, and by 1861 Bishop Hill Colony was dead. The settlers spread out, and today's Bishop Hill was founded two miles to the south.

The old site is now a State Historic Site with 16 of the original buildings having been restored. There are also museums depicting various facets of life in the old Swedish commune and 25 shops selling handicrafts and antiques.

GALENA (Jo Daviess Co.)

class E (NR)-lead mining

In the northwest corner of Illinois, fifteen miles east of Dubuque, Iowa.

Galena is NOT a ghost town, but an active,

historic community with a population of 3647. In the early to mid 1800s, Galena was center of the nation's lead mining industry. The region also includes southwestern Wisconsin (see Chapter 10).

In 1816, the first load of lead ore from the Fever (Galena) River headed south, and the rush to the mines began. In 1819 a trading post was established at the site that became Galena. In 1826 a town was laid out by Lt. Martin Thomas, the official US Government mine agent. By the 1830s, Galena was a major commercial center, and in 1841 the city of 2225 people was incorporated.

1845 was the peak year for the mines with 54 million pounds of lead produced, representing over 80% of the country's total for that year! Nearly all the lead passed through the town and onto the docks for shipment to St. Louis. Through the 1850s, lead production slowed, but Galena focused on being the region's number one mercantile center as well, so the economy remained positive.

In 1854 a major fire ripped through town, and later that same year the railroad arrived. This killed steamboat transportation, diluting Galena's importance as a port city. A second conflagration tore through town in 1856, and by the time the ashes cooled, the city council had passed an ordinance requiring all new buildings to be built of brick or stone.

In 1858 Galena reached its peak population of 14,000. With the onset of the Civil War, most of the traditional trade routes to the south were blocked, so Galena's economy sputtered. It faded rapidly, losing its place as the center for the lead mining industry, as a transportation center, and as a regional marketing center.

After the war ended, the town slipped into a century long reverie, just barely alive, but enough to prevent demolition of its historic structures. During the 1960s and early 1970s, there was an influx of ex-city folk who came, liked what they saw, and stayed. The town spruced up, and today Galena's historic district is rated the best example of Victorian architecture in the Midwest. 85% of its downtown buildings are listed on the National Register.

NAUVOO (Hancock Co.)

class E-Mormon "boom town"

28 miles southwest of Burlington, Iowa, at the present town of Nauvoo.

In 1839, Joseph Smith and several thousand faithful followers of the Church of Jesus Christ of the Later Day Saints (Mormons) settled in the tiny farming community of Nauvoo, trying to escape the persecution that continually dogged them. Suddenly Nauvoo was the largest town in the state with an 1840 population of 8000.

In 1844, Smith and his brother were murdered, and the Mormon farming community was wracked with dissention. Other non-Mormons in the community put pressure on them to leave, so in 1846, Brigham Young gathered the faithful followers, and they began their trek to the west.

In 1848, vandals burned the unfinished temple, and then in 1849, a group of French Icarians settled and opened a socialistic commune, which lasted until 1858, when it was disbanded.

Today (New) Nauvoo is a peaceful community of 1100 people, and has many sites that hearken back to the boom years when it was the headquarters for the LDS church.

Other ghost towns in Illinois include...

ALPINE (Cook Co.)

class B-railroad town

30 miles southwest of Chicago and three miles south of Orland Park. This suburban ghost town was founded as a Wabash Line Railroad station in 1891. In 1910

the town peaked with a blacksmith shop, feed store, two story general store/dance hall, three saloons, and a railroad depot. In 1912 fire destroyed the store and two saloons, putting the town in a tailspin. By WWII it was a vacant site.

KASKASKIA (Randolph Co.)
class B-state capital

On a Mississippi River island, 15 miles north of Perryville, Missouri. When Illinois became a state in 1818, Kaskaskia was designated the state capital. The capital was removed to Vandalia in 1819, and Kaskaskia quickly faded.

NEW SALEM (Menard Co.)
class C/F (restored)-crossroads settlement

This 1830s crossroads settlement had a carding mill, cooperage, gristmill, sawmill, school and tavern, among other structures. It died after nearby Petersburg was made county seat in 1839.

Located on SH 97, two miles south of Petersburg, New Salem is now a 600 acre historic site consisting of 23 re-constructed buildings showing what the town looked like when Abraham Lincoln lived there from 1831-1837.

(Old) SHAWNEETOWN (Gallatin Co.)
class Db-riverport

During the early 1800s, Shawneetown was a bustling Ohio River port, shipping center, and salt mining town, but continual floods caused the residents to relocate to higher ground, which led to the founding of NEW Shawneetown. The old site is still home for 356 people. It is on SH 13, three miles east of New Shawneetown (pop 1576) and 23 miles east of Harrisburg.

For the researcher...

ALTON PRISONER OF WAR CAMP (Madison Co... Civil War POW camp), DENROCK (Whiteside Co...on the Rock River), FAYVILLE (Alexander Co...ferry to Commerce, MO), SELLER'S LANDING (Hardin Co...1831-1851 milling town), YOUNGSTOWN (Warren Co...1980 population of 40).

Indiana

CONRAD (Newton Co.)

class B-rural town

Along SH 41 and the RR, just south of Lake Village, approximately 40 miles south of Gary.

Founded in 1908, the small town of 200 people included a church, concrete block factory, hotel, post office, railroad depot, and a school. The streets were named after various members of the founding Conrad family.

A major fire swept through the town, and it never recovered. It is now just a rubble strewn site.

GOLD CREEK (Morgan Co.)

class B-gold mining

Between SH 39 and SH 67, 25 miles southwest of Indianapolis.

In the early 1900s gold was found in streamside glacial gravels southwest of Indianapolis. A small mining camp popped up at the creek site, but placer recoveries of $0.25 to $1.50 a day didn't encourage many people, and the camp folded.

Other Morgan County mining camps were located on HIGHLAND CREEK, LAMB'S CREEK and SYCAMORE CREEK. Sycamore and Lamb's Creeks were first mined during the 1850s by California Gold Rush returnees, but the poor glacial gravels frustrated them, and they moved on. All three creeks were worked again in the early 1900s.

HINDOSTAN (Martin Co.)
class B-county seat

Along the East Fork of the White River, several miles southwest of Shoals, which is at the junction of US 50/150, 21 miles east of Washington.

Hindostan was founded around 1814 by Frederick Sholts. It became an important stage stopping place, as well as the county seat. It contained a grist mill, saw mill and a tavern.

In June, 1828 a plague of some kind swept through town, killing many of the citizens, and sending the rest on a panic to get out of town. The county seat was transferred to Mt. Pleasant, and the site of Hindostan became a true ghost town. Ruins include foundation pits, a restored church and a modern park near the site.

Other ghost towns in Indiana include...

ENTERPRISE (Spencer Co.)
class Da-riverport

Six miles southeast of Hatfield. This once thriving Ohio River port was founded in 1862. Evansville, down river eventually drew the steamer traffic away and Enterprise died. In the 1980s there were four people living here.

LEAVENWORTH (Crawford Co.)
class B-riverport

Located along the river flats of the Ohio River two

miles south of I-64 at EXIT 92 and 13 miles west of Corydon. The entire town was relocated to the bluffs above the river in 1937 after a bad flood destroyed most of the town. The old site was abandoned.

PERTH (Clay Co.)
class C-coal mining

Located about five miles north of Brazil, this old coal camp was settled in the 1880s, and died in the 1930s. It had a number of businesses, including saloons.

SPRING MILL (Lawrence Co.)
class C/F(restored-SHP-$)-grist mill village

On SH 60, several miles east of Mitchell. This tiny 1815 era trading post/village has been restored, and consists of an apothecary, boot shop, water powered grist mill, hatmaker shop, limekiln ruins, post office, and sawmill.

SULPHUR (Crawford Co.)
class Da-spa/resort

A large 100-room grand hotel with bath houses, bowling alley, post office, store, and bottling works for the sulphur charged water was the extent of the tiny town in the late 1800s. It was located near the present town of Sulphur, which is just south of I-64 at EXIT 80, 28 miles east of Dale.

For the researcher...

BEAN BLOSSOM CREEK (Brown Co...gold mining area), BLACKFORD (Posey Co...1815-1818 boom), NEW BALTIMORE (Posey Co...1837-1900 riverport), OLD CALE (Martin Co...a farmer's hidden cache.) WINFIELD (Posey Co...1838-1858)

Ohio

BUCKEYE FURNACE (Jackson Co.)
class C/F (restored-$)-iron furnace village

On CR 58, 10 miles east of Jackson, and 7.5 miles southeast of Wellston.

Buckeye Furnace was originally built in 1851, and operated until 1894. A visitor center and museum outline the history of the site and its iron furnaces. The complex includes the casting shed, charcoal storage building, charging house, engine house and company store, and restored remains of the charcoal powered iron furnace.

FORT AMANDA (Auglaize Co.)
class B-military post

A War of 1812 military post on SH 198, nine miles northwest of Wapakoneta. There is a monument and picnic facility at the site.

FORT MEIGS (Wood Co.)
class C (restored-$)-military post

Located on SH 65, along the south bank of the Maumee River, just southwest of Perrysburg.

During the winter of 1812-1813, this army post was established on a ten acre site. It consisted of barracks, block houses, and a barricade. Shortly after it was established, the British attacked it, but with help from General William Henry Harrison's troops, the fort was spared. After the War of 1812 ended, it was abandoned.

The old post has been reconstructed, and is one of the largest log forts in the country.

ZOAR (Tuscarawas Co.)

class C/F restored ($)-German communal village

Located on SH 212, 2.5 miles southeast of I-77 at EXIT 93, northwest of the existing town of Zoarville.

In 1817, a group of German separatists founded this communal village. It was a simple Christian agrarian commune, and the members labored together to make it work. Despite that, it disbanded in 1898, and the site has been restored by the state historical society.

The site consists of several museums and craft shops as well.

For the researcher...

FORT JEFFERSON (Darke Co...an 1791 military post), INDEPENDENCE (Defiance Co...a near ghost town in 1984), NEW GATTANGEN (Guernsey Co...1836 town NE of Senecaville), PRATTSVILLE (Vinton Co...1980 pop of 35), ZONE (Fulton Co...1980 population of 25).

Dust in the Wind

The Northeast

The northeastern states are usually not considered much when a person thinks of ghost towns, yet each has many of its own. Compared to the western states, what these states lack in quantity of tangible remains, they make up for in diversity and age. This is the oldest part of the country, and with over 400 years of settlement, the number of sites is staggering. Serious research can reveal hundreds or thousands of sites, and for those who enjoy that facet of ghost towning, the possibilities are nearly endless. The ghost towns of the northeast are not as visible as those in the West or Mid-west, but they are indeed there. It just takes a little extra effort to find them.

It is here that many of the United States's oldest ghost towns are located. Many of the remaining locations with buildings have been restored, and may be part of a state or federal park, or a private site with an admission charge. This doesn't lessen their importance in the history of the region, but sometimes can jade the dedicated ghost towner.

Old mining, milling, and manufacturing communities have lived and died and been swallowed up by forest and farm. Logging and railroad towns have disappeared, old coastal fishing villages and riverports have faded from memory. Throw in the crossroads communities and taverns, and the Northeast looks real bright for the serious ghost town chaser.

There are thousands of ghost towns in the northeast!

Chapter Twelve

Delaware

FORT DELAWARE (New Castle Co.)
class C/F (SP-$)-military post

On Pea Patch Island, in the middle of the Delaware River, just east of Delaware City.

This stone masonry fort was built in 1859. During the Civil War it was used as a prisoner of war camp, with 12,000 Southern troops housed here in frame barracks. During the Spanish American War, the fort was fully garrisoned, but shut down after that war ended.

It is now a state park, and access is via boat.

OLD FURNACE (Sussex Co.)
class B-iron furnace

Shown on the official state roadmap along a branch of Deep Creek, about five miles east of Seaford. Nothing is shown in the Rand McNally Commercial Atlas and Marketing Guide.

ZWAANENDAEL (Sussex Co.)
class A-Dutch colonial town

Southwest of Lewes, near the junction of SH 1 and US 9.

This was the first major Dutch colonial town, and

was founded in 1631 and destroyed by Indians in 1632. When it was rebuilt, it was rebuilt closer to Delaware Bay. This second site is known today as Lewes.

For the researcher...

ALLEE HOUSE ("Kent Co.." Country House inn built in 1753), ANDREWSVILLE (Kent Co...1980 population of 30), duPONT COLONY (New Castle Co...1802 colony founded by E.I. duPont.), FORT CHRISTINA (New Castle Co...original site of Wilmington), ROBINSONVILLE (Sussex Co...SW of Lewes).

Maryland

CATOCTIN FURNACE (Frederick Co.)

class Da-iron furnace

Located on SH 806, just off US 15, three miles south of Thurmont.

The furnace was built by James and Thomas Johnson between 1774 and 1776. They produced household items, pig iron, shells for 10" mortars, and tools. Through the early 1800s, the furnace changed hands several times. In the 1850s the community consisted of three furnaces, a company store, grist mill, homes, railroad, and a sawmill.

By 1903 the furnaces had shut down and the town faded. Today's Catoctin is a small community just south of the original iron forge town. Remains at the furnace site include stone walls, furnace ruins, ruins of the ironmaster's mansion, and a reconstructed casting shed.

Restored casting house and furnace at Catoctin Furnace, MD

FORT FOOTE (Prince Georges Co.)
class B-military post

Along the east bank of the Potomac River, in Fort Foote Park, about a mile and a half west of Indian Head Highway (SH 210) a mile and a half south of I-95/495.

Fort Foote overlooks the Potomac River shipping lanes, and was the site of several 15" Rodman Cannons that could shoot 400 pound cannonballs four miles. It was completed on June 25, 1865, and named after flag officer Andrew Hull Foote, a Union Naval hero that was killed on February 14, 1862 at Fort Donelson, TN. It was only occupied a short time.

Today the remains of the old fort are rapidly being reclaimed by vegetation, but the crumbling concrete and earth bulwarks which were designed to protect the men and guns from enemy ship fire are still found in the overgrown tangle of greenery.

Rodman Cannon bases at Fort Foote, MD

FORT FREDERICK (Washington Co.)

class C/F (restored-SP)-military post

Overlooking the Potomac River, south of SH 56, just east of Big Pool, 16 miles west of Hagerstown.

In 1756, the huge stone-walled fort was erected as a major defense for Maryland during the French and Indian Wars of 1754-1763. Shaped like a four pointed star, it has two large barracks buildings that were built to house 200 soldiers. During the American Revolution it served as a refuge for local settlers, and in 1779 acted as a prison camp for captured Hessian soldiers.

On Christmas Day, 1861, the old fort saw its only military engagement, a brief skirmish with Confederate forces.

In 1922, the state of Maryland purchased the site, and during the 1930s, it was a CCC restoration project. Again in 1976 restoration work was done.

FORT WASHINGTON (Prince Georges Co.)
class C/F (restored-NP-$)-military post

Overlooking the Potomac River, almost directly opposite Mount Vernon, seven miles south of Oxon Hill, west of SH 210.

Fort Washington was constructed to protect Washington, D.C. and was part of the system of Coastal Defense Forts being built to protect the entire east coast. Construction began in 1808, and on December 1, 1809 it was completed. When the British marched on Washington on August 19, 1814, they went around the fort. The next day, Captain Samuel Dyson retreated and destroyed the fort and all its munitions, rather than surrender it to the British.

Inside the compound at Fort Washington, MD

A month later, construction began on a new fort, and it was completed on October 2, 1824. In the mid 1840s it was remodeled and strengthened, and emplacements for 88 cannons were added.

In 1861, with the Civil War looming, the fort's position was extremely important. Since it was the only fort protecting Washington, D.C., other forts were built around the capital to protect it to avoid a repeat of 1814.

Administration buildings at Fort Washington, MD

During the Spanish American War (1898) more batteries, including four 15" Rodman Cannons and armor piercing mortars, were added, making attack by river almost suicidal.

It remained an active duty post until 1946 when it was decommissioned. Many buildings were removed, but the remaining buildings were preserved as a National Park.

NEW GERMANY (Garrett Co.)

class A-milling center

Located in New Germany State Park in the far western tip of the state, 25 miles west of Cumberland.

John Swauger established a sawmill and grist mill in the mid 1800s. The grist mill operated until 1859, and was powered by water from the 13 acre lake created by damming Poplar Lick Run. The sawmill continued in use until 1890. Other sawmills were set up, and the area became a major sawmilling center.

Nothing remains of this old milling center, and the area is a popular state park.

Other ghost towns in Maryland include...

GREAT FALLS TAVERN/MARYLAND GOLD MINE (Montgomery Co.)

class B(mine)/D (tavern)-mine and tavern

These sites are located at the Great Falls of the Potomac, west of Potomac. The gold mines are about a mile southeast of the tavern. They were worked in the 1800s, and the tavern was an important stopping point on the C & O Canal. It was first used as a lock house (1831), then a tavern. It is currently used as a visitor center for the C & O Canal NHP.

ROCK RUN (Harford Co)

class C/F (restored-SP)-grist mill community

Along the Susquehanna River, southeast of Darlington.

The original grist mill was built in 1794 by John Stump. It was the center of a thriving little community that included a post office, spring house, toll house, carriage barn, and several homes. The settlement lasted until the early 1900s.

For the researcher...

HARFORD FURNACE (Harford Co...old furnace town), MAPLE VIEW (Carroll Co...1980 population of 15), Civil War Prisoner of War Camp (St Mary's Co... on Point Lookout), PROVIDENCE (Anne Arundel Co... colony established in 1649), STAFFORD (Harford Co... white flint mining town).

New Jersey

BATSTO (Burlington Co.)

class C/F (restored-SHS-$)-iron forge village

In Wharton State Forest, on SSH 542, nine miles east of Hammonton.

A major bog iron forge village that was founded in 1766. It supplied material to the colonists in their battles with the British during the Revolutionary War. The charcoal that fueled the furnaces was produced from locally felled trees.

After the war ended, the brickyards, glassworks, a grist mill, iron forge and sawmill contributed to the local economy, and the town grew to a population of about 1000.

Coal powered furnaces were more efficient, and as they grew in popularity, the charcoal powered furnaces declined. Batsto's charcoal powered forges became unprofitable, and by 1848 they shut down. The town followed suit, and in 1874 a fire destroyed half of the nearly abandoned town.

In 1954 Wharton State Forest was established, and the town was partially restored, and is a designated State Historic Site. Some of the buildings that have been rebuilt include the ironmaster's mansion, the furnace, the grist mill, and the sawmill.

SPEEDWELL VILLAGE (Morris Co.)

class C/F (restored-$)-iron factory village

Just off US 202, about a mile north of Morristown, west of New York City.

In 1767, Zachariah Fairchild operated a sawmill across the Whippany River from an iron forge operated by John Johnson. In 1808 Stephen Vail, and two others bought a half interest in the location, and the Speedwell Iron Works were in business.

Vail poured his money and energy into the site, and despite struggling for a few years, eventually bought out his partners. He focused on manufacturing of products from iron pigs, rather than the actual smelting process. In 1818, one of his largest projects was the engine for the first transatlantic steam ship, the S.S. Savannah, among others. He also supplied parts for the Baldwin Locomotive Works in Philadelphia. In 1837, Stephen's son Alfred was one of Samuel Morse's helpers, and he rented them the unused cotton factory building. Here Morse perfected the telegraph.

The village included the foundry, machine shop, sawmill, cotton factory, the Vail home, workers cottages and a hotel (Eagle Hotel). In 1844, George Vail took over from his father, and Speedwell operated successfully until it closed in 1873.

In 1908 fire destroyed many buildings on the site. In 1955 Speedwell site passed into private hands, then in 1967 the site was purchased by a group called The

Speedwell Village. In 1975, the cotton factory was declared a National Historic Landmark, and the entire Speedwell site has been opened to the public.

The ironworks are marked by the crumbling stone walls of workers' cottages and workshops, as well as standing buildings spared by the fire of 1908. Restoration is ongoing.

STERLING HILL ZINC MINE (Sussex Co.)
class C-zinc mining

Just north of Ogdensburg, which is on SSH 517, four miles north of Sparta.

This old zinc mining camp was started originally by Dutch settlers in the 1640s or 1650s. In 1756, a British gentleman, the Earl of Sterling, worked the mines, but couldn't make it pay. In 1913, the New Jersey Zinc Co. operated the site profitably for 70 years, finally closing down in early 1983.

During its peak, 500 miners worked this mine, which was the third largest in the country. The shafts are 2600 feet deep. The site is now a mining museum.

Other ghost towns in New Jersey include...

HANOVER FURNACE (Burlington Co.)
class B-iron furnace village

Four miles east of Brown Mills, which is on SSH 530 south of Ft. Dix. This was a bog iron community dating to the mid and late 1700s. It may have reached a population of a thousand, and consisted of 200 buildings.

ONGS HAT (Burlington Co.)
class B-tavern/crossroads settlement

Four miles east of Burrs Mill, then two miles northwest

on Pemberton Road, at the westernmost point of the Lebanon State Forest, in the Pine Barrens. A tavern was opened here around 1800. It is said to have been a wild place during Prohibition, and the town was still operating as late as the 1930s. Only rubble remains.

PAHAQUARRY COPPER MINES (Warren Co.)

class B-copper mining

In the northwestern part of the county, northeast of Stroudsburg, PA. These were the first commercial copper mines in what is now the USA. The Dutch heard about the copper from local Indians, and in the 1640s the Dutch began to mine the ore. The copper was excavated and processed on site, and then shipped to Esopus, (now called Kingston, NY.), for refining.

TRENTON FERRY/ROYAL OAK INN (Warren Co.)

class C-ferry/roadside tavern

Located in Bloomsburg, along the Musconetcong River.

Trenton Ferry was opened about 1726, and in 1753 a tavern was built at the ferry to serve customers. It became a popular stage stop, but by 1797 the tavern was gone.

For the researcher...

ATSION (Burlington Co...1776 bog iron village), BODINE'S TAVERN (Burlington Co...early 1830s tavern and gathering spot), INDIAN KING TAVERN (Camden Co...1750 roadhouse/tavern), PASADENA (Ocean Co...late 1800s clay pottery manufacturing village), TOPANEMUS (Monmouth Co...founded in 1685 by Quakers).

Dust in the Wind

Chapter Thirteen

New York

ELLIS ISLAND (New York Co.)

class C/F (restored-NM)-immigration station

Located in Upper New York Bay, southwest of the southern tip of Manhattan Island. Usually reached by the Statue of Liberty/Ellis Island Ferry ($) from the south tip of Manhattan Island at the Castle Clinton ferry landing, or from Liberty State Park, New Jersey.

Ellis Island was an extremely busy, self contained island community. On April 11, 1890, the island was designated an official immigration station, and on January 1, 1892, it opened. Over the next 62 years, Ellis Island was the gateway to the United States for over 50% of all immigrants.

On June 14, 1897, the building complex burned, and the island was closed until December 17, 1900, when it reopened. In 1924, mass migrations to the US ended, and Ellis Island was used as a deportation center as well as immigration center, although on a much smaller scale than the 1900-1924 era.

During the 1917-1919 and 1941-1954 periods it was also used as a detention center for suspected enemy aliens. Finally on November 29, 1954, Ellis Island closed its doors, after admitting 16,000,000 immigrants to American shores. In 1965, it was added to the Statue of Liberty

National Monument, and in 1976 opened to the public for visits.

The island was closed again in 1984 for a $156 million renovation and restoration project. On September 10, 1990 it reopened. It now consists of a fully restored complex of buildings with museums, exhibits and interpretive displays.

Did your ancestors pass through here? Ellis Island, NY

FORT LEVIS (St. Lawrence Co.)

class B-French military post

On Chimney Island (Isle Royal), about 3.5 miles from Ogdensburg, in the St. Lawrence River.

The small island was occupied by the French in the late 1750s, and Fort Levis was built by Marquis de Levis, in 1759. It was garrisoned the next year, and remained a French stronghold until the British drove them out. After the British were chased out by the Americans, the old fort was destroyed, and for many years nothing but a chimney remained. Today, only rubble remains of the old fort.

HOGENCAMP (Orange Co.)

class B-iron mining

Located in Harriman State Park, northwest of SH 210/ Seven Lakes Parkway interchange and east of I-87.

This small iron mining camp was clustered around the Hogencamp Mine, which was owned by Robert and Peter Parrott (who also owned the nearby Greenwood Furnace). The mine was operated from 1861-1885, and had six adits. The orebody was 60' deep, 250' long, and from 12-15' wide.

The mining camp had 20 homes, barns, a combination dance hall/saloon, school, and a store. Nothing but rubble remains.

MOUNT LEBANON (Columbia Co.)

class E/F (boarding school)-Shaker colony

On US 20, near New Lebanon, in the northeast corner of the county.

This was a self sufficient, late 1800s Shaker Colony. The Shakers were an offshoot of the Quakers, and formed small colonies wherever they settled. This particular colony is one of the largest that has remaining buildings. It is currently in use as a boarding school (Darrow School).

When the colony was still alive, the 25 buildings housed a couple barns, granary, infirmary, an iron forge, medicine shop (drug store), milk house, two meeting houses, schoolhouse, sheep barn, tannery, wash house, and a number of cottages.

Other ghost towns in New York include...

GIBSONVILLE (Livingston Co.)
class B-mill town

At the north end of Letchworth State Park, west of Mt. Morris. This rubbled site was once an old paper mill town with a hotel, several stores, and 40-50 homes.

ORAMEL (Allegany Co.)
class Db-shipping center

The tiny, sleepy hamlet of Oramel (1980 population of 150) sits in the northwest part of the county along the Genesee River. During the 1800s, this town was a busy port on the Genesee Valley Canal. Its mile long canal-front docks supported the town of 1000 people, along with the usual assortment of hotels, boarding houses and stores.

PORTAGE (Livingston Co.)
class B-resort area

South of Letchworth Park, near present Portageville. This resort area boomed in the early 1900s when excursion trains arrived regularly. During the 1930s, travelers found less expensive places to visit, the trains stopped coming, and the town folded. The few remaining residents moved to nearby Portageville. Time has taken its toll, and nothing remains but rubble.

For the researcher...

BLACK HORSE INN (??? Co...Old 1791 inn on the King's Highway), CIVIL WAR TRAINING CAMPS (Various counties... training facilities for NY Volunteer regiments), EAST WINDHAM (Greene Co...tiny town with 25 people), KNOTLIMB (Orange Co...old village whose location has been forgotten), WATERBORO (Chautauqua Co.... "extinct village" six miles west of Randolph).

Pennsylvania

AZILUM (Bradford Co.)

class C/F (restored-$)-French village

Three miles east of SH 187 at a point 10 miles east of Towanda.

During 1793, French citizens escaping the turmoil of the French Revolution settled here. The community consisted of about 50 log structures, some of which included a tavern and shops. It was situated on the river to have direct access to Philadelphia.

The settlers farmed the region with success, but within ten years most had moved on, and by 1810, the place had been deserted, and was falling to ruin.

In the early 1990s it was undergoing restoration work, and a number of exhibits were open.

HOPEWELL FURNACE (Berks Co.)

class C/F (restored-NHS-$)-iron forge village

35 air miles northwest of Philadelphia, just off SH 345, 6.5 miles northeast of Elverson.

In the fall of 1743, William Bird erected a forge near Birdsboro, which he called Hopewell Forge. By the spring of 1744 pig iron was being produced. He died in 1761, and the forges were taken over by his 22 year old son, Mark.

In 1770 rich iron deposits were found about 10 miles south of the forge, and in 1771 Hopewell Furnace was erected on French Creek. By 1772 the charcoal powered furnace was in full blast. Some of the items produced included pig iron, cannons, pots, stoveplates, tools, window sash weights, and shot for use by the Continental Army and Navy.

After the war ended, Bird tried to expand his holdings, and stretched his finances too far. The economic recession of the 1780s broke him, and in 1788 Bird sold Hopewell and his other properties to repay various obligations.

The furnace was now under new ownership, but due to litigation and major repairs, it wasn't until 1816 that the furnace began to pay for itself again.

Restored casting shed and furnace at Hopewell Furnace, PA

The facility's production skyrocketed. Between 1825 and 1850, the operation averaged 1000 tons of pig iron annually. A village of 1000 people had grown up around the furnace, which included the furnaces, a blacksmith shop, company store and office, homes for the workers and their families, the ironmaster's mansion, livery stable/barn, schoolhouse, and wheelwright.

By 1850, coal-powered furnaces out produced the

Ruins of anthracite coal furnace at Hopewell Furnace, PA

charcoal furnaces, and activity declined until the Civil War, when there was a brief flurry of activity. Decline again set in until June 15, 1883, when the furnaces shut down.

There was some spotty activity until 1913.

In 1935 the old village stood deserted except a few folks living in run down cabins. The Federal government purchased the site, and in 1946, the historic old community was made a historic site and reconstruction began.

Today the restored village is one of the best examples of a mid-1800s iron forge community.

PITHOLE CITY (Venango Co.)

class B ($)-oil boom town

On a small road 2.3 miles east of SH 227 at a point 1.5 miles north of Plummer.

On January 15, 1865 news of the oil strike on

Pithole Creek reached the outside. A massive rush to the site ensued, and by September, Pithole City had 15,000 people, and is said to have had 50 hotels among many businesses, which included an opera house, six restaurants, two banks, and scores of other businesses.

By November the wells slowed, and within two years the site was abandoned. Fires destroyed many buildings, and the rest were torn down for use as firewood. By 1890 the site had been reclaimed by nature.

Today the old site is nothing but a collection of foundations, cellar holes and rubble. A visitor center is at the site, and walking tours are offered.

Other ghost towns in Pennsylvania include...

BETULA (McKean Co.)
class Da-lumbering center

Just west of SH 46, about 12 miles south southeast of Smethport. This was a major lumbering center in the early 1900s, and had a population of 1500.

CORNWALL FURNACE (Lebanon Co.)
class C/F (restored-$)-iron forge village

On SH 419, 5 miles south of Lebanon. The forge and community were active from 1742-1883. Some of the products included farm tools, kitchenware, and stoveplates. During the Revolutionary War, it also made cannons and shot. The site has been restored and a number of buildings are open for visitors.

ECKLEY (Luzern Co.)
class Da/F (restored-$)-coal mining

On SH 940, 9 miles east-northeast of Hazelton. This anthracite coal mining town began in 1854, and by 1870 had a population over 1000 people. By 1990 that had been reduced to 80. It had stores, churches and schools. The state purchased the property in 1971, and the village is now a living history museum.

MINA (Potter Co.)
class B-lumber center

This old lumbering center was located five miles southwest of Coudersport, and in 1900 had about 1500 people. It was a busy town with blacksmiths, post office, restaurants, school, and stores. By 1980 all that remained were a few foundations, cellar holes, and the old railroad depot serving as a cattle shelter.

For the researcher...

BROOKSTON (Forest Co...1870s railroad town), ARRANDSVILLE (Clinton Co...brick manufacturing town), HICKS RUN (Cameron Co...early 1900s lumber camp), LAQUIN CITY (Bradford Co...lumbering town with 100+ buildings), WHISKEY RUN (Indiana Co...a town shrouded in mystery).

Dust in the Wind

Chapter Fourteen

Connecticut

DUDLEYTOWN (Litchfield Co.)
class B-farming

In the hills southwest of Cornwall, and northeast of Cornwall Bridge.

This old farming town above the Housatonic River was established in 1747, but the high hills around the site kept extra sunlight out, and the farms did poorly due to thin soil, high winds, and lack of water.

It was claimed that the "Dudleytown Curse" prevented affluence, and was claimed to have supernatural connections. Those connections didn't want a town to be on the site. It is claimed by some, that every seven years the curse would strike, and somebody would die of unusual causes. Curse or no curse, the last citizen left in 1900.

Remains include cellar holes, rock walls, and rubble.

NEW GATE PRISON/
SIMSBURY COPPER MINE (Hartford Co.)
class C/F (restored-NHL-$)-prison/copper mine

On Newgate Rd., about 2 miles north of SH 20, midway between Granby and East Granby.

Copper ore was discovered and first worked here in 1707. It ran from 12-50% copper, but due to limited knowledge of copper mining, and refining that had to be done in England, the mine ceased operation in 1773, shortly after the Colony of Connecticut purchased the site for use as a prison. The prisoners were used to work the mines until it closed. Later they were used to manufacture nails and shoes, and the underground workings were used for cells.

Three years later, in October, 1776, the prison was designated the first state prison in the new country, and from 1775 through 1782, it was used to hold captured British soldiers and British sympathizers. In September, 1827 the prison was abandoned, and the prisoners moved to a new facility in Wethersfield.

The state purchased the site from a private party in 1968, and in 1972 a stairway was built to allow access to the mine for tourists. Today the mine is a National Historic Landmark, is listed on the National Register, and is a state historic landmark.

Other ghost towns in Connecticut include...

MERROW (Tolland Co)

class Db-manufacturing

On SH 32, 2 miles north of Mansfield Depot, 13 miles east of Manchester, this old manufacturing town has faded from the days when its mills bustled with activity. Remains of this tiny community of 250 people include many abandoned buildings and ruins.

MILLINGTON GREEN (Middlesex Co.)

class B-lumber

An old lumbering community in the eastern part of the county, midway between Middletown and New London. The lumber was cut and sent to shipbuilders along the Connecticut River. All that remains are cellar holes and rubble.

POQUETANUCK (New London Co.)
class Db-seaport

A bustling Thames River port and trading center that has faded from its glory days in the 1800s. It is at the junction of SH 117 and SH 2A, five miles southeast of Norwich. Many ruins and unoccupied buildings remain.

WELLS WOODS (Tolland Co.)
class B-farming

On Wells Wood Road, east of Hebron, and a half mile south of SH 66. All that remain of this old hamlet are cellar holes, stone walls and granite foundation stones.

For the researcher...

ALLYN'S POINT (New London Co...coal shipping port), BURRVILLE (Litchfield Co...iron foundry town), GREYSTONE (Litchfield Co...manufacturing town), Mt. RIGA (Litchfield Co...iron forge community that faded after 1847), SOUTHVILLE (Fairfield Co...once prosperous manufacturing community).

Massachusetts

GEORGE'S ISLAND (Suffolk Co.)
class C-military post

One of the outermost islands in Boston Harbor.

The history of this small island dates back to 1690 when an English fleet used it as a staging point for an attack on Canada. The French occupied the site for a short time in 1778.

In 1826 construction of a seawall began, and in 1833, Fort Warren was established. By 1861, it was an active post occupied by various units of Massachusetts militia units. Later that year, the fort held several hundred Confederate prisoners of war. In 1895, construction of several new officers quarters took place, followed in 1900 with additional troop barracks. By the beginning of WW I, the post held over 1500 soldiers. It was decommissioned in 1928. Again, during WWII it was reactivated, but has been vacant since.

The site is now part of Boston Harbor Islands State Park.

NORTH PEPPERELL (Middlesex Co.)
class B-manufacturing

Located north of Pepperell, along the Nissitissett River.

During the early 1800s, North Pepperell boasted a grist mill, post office, sawmill, brick school house, store and tavern. A dam provided a steady supply of water and power, and the local farms were very productive.

After the War of 1812, an old woman moved into a cabin on the outskirts, and she was accused of being a witch. After being physically attacked, she is claimed to have put a curse on the town, and then disappeared. (Shades of Dudleytown!)

The people ignored her curse, but in the mid 1800s the shoe shop burned. During the next 25 years four mills were lost to fire, the last burning in 1884. A number of people died odd and gruesome deaths, and 70 years after the curse was supposedly made, the town was deserted.

Today, nothing but foundations and rubble remain.

SKINNERSVILLE (Hampshire Co.)
class A-silk manufacturing

Along Mill River, and SH 9, a mile southeast of Williamsburg.

The huge brick Usquomonk Silk Mill was the largest manufacturing plant in the small river town. On Saturday May 16, 1874, the factory, the village and four people disappeared when a massive flood washed down the valley from a broken dam three miles above Williamsburg. The dam was built in 1865 to supply a controlled amount of water for the various manufacturing mills along the river, and its failure swept 143 people to their deaths, and destroyed four communities. Skinnersville is the only one that has not been rebuilt.

Other ghost towns in Massachusetts include...

BANCROFT (Hampshire Co.)
class Da-milling

Along the east bank of the West Branch Westfield River. This former community was the site of the Berkshire Tissue Mills, which closed in 1894. There was also a meeting house, offices and a school.

DAVIS (Franklin Co.)
class B-pyrite mining

An abandoned pyrite mining town that was active from 1882-1910. In 1937 the only evidence that a large community existed was the blacksmith shop and some 150 cellar holes located 2.4 miles north of Charlemont.

For the researcher...

DOGTOWN (Essex Co...deserted 1719-1830 village), Mt. WACHUSETT MOUNTAIN HOUSE (Worcester Co... stage stop/tavern), OLD FURNACE (Worcester Co...iron furnace), QUINAPOXET (Worcester Co... (rubbled site of once prosperous mill town), TANTISQUES LEAD MINE (Worcester Co...1638-1900 lead mine).

Rhode Island

BEACH POND CCC CAMP (Kent Co.)

class A-CCC camp

In Beach Pond State Park, near where SH 165 exits the west side of the state.

Established in early 1930s, and by 1937 consisted of 14 buildings. This small work camp also had a canteen where the workers could purchase sundries such as candy, beer, and cigarettes.

DURFEE HILL GOLD MINE (Providence Co.)

class C-gold mining

Operation of this gold mine began in late 1700s, but an underground a stream of water was hit, shutting down the mine until the late 1800s. At that time ore valued at $2.50 per ton was mined. Around 1900 a pair of investors salted the mine and sold $100,000 in stock, and then disappeared.

The mine has never really lived up to its expectations. It is located on Durfee Hill Rd, north of Ponaganset Reservoir, four air miles southeast of West Glocester.

EAGLEVILLE (Newport Co.)

class B-milling

1.6 miles northeast of Tiverton, which is six miles south of Fall River, MA. This once flourishing milling center began in 1827 when the cotton and woolen mills were erected. In 1861 fire destroyed the woolen mill, and the village began to fade. By 1937 only one house remained in this deserted village.

FOSTER GOLD MINE (Providence Co.)

class C-gold mining

On Harrington Rd, just North of Moosup Valley, several miles southwest of Foster Center.

From the 1700s to the early 1900s this old gold mine was worked off and on. Like the Durfee Hill Mine, it never really paid back its investors.

PERRYVILLE (Washington Co.)

class B-rural community

On SH 110, just north of US 1, about five miles east of Charlestown. In 1937, the town had six houses, and in 1990 it had 50 people.

For the researcher...

ARNOLD'S POINT FORT (Newport Co...at the north end of Rhode "Island"), BUTTS HILL FORT (Newport Co...just north of Portsmouth), FRENCHTOWN (Kent Co...Huguenot Settlement), PIDGE TAVERN (Providence Co...old tavern), SOUTH FERRY (Washington Co...ferry landing town).

Dust in the Wind

Chapter Fifteen

Maine

PEMAQUID (Lincoln Co.)
class Db (SHS)-colony/fishing

On SH 130, ten miles south of Damariscotta.

In 1608 the British colonists of Pemaquid were run out by the local Indians. They returned, and by 1620 it was a thriving fishing community. It was burned in 1675, and captured by the French in 1689.

Today this historic old community barely clings to life with a 1990 population of 125. The old colonial site is a State Historic Site, and contains the excavated remains of the old colony. A museum ($) details the site's history.

PENTAGOET (Hancock Co.)
class B-French colonial settlement

On the bank of the Bagaduce River on east side of Penobscot Bay near Castine.

The first settlement at the site was a trading post that may have been established in the early 1600s. In 1635, the French forced the British out of the region, and in 1654, the British returned the favor. In 1670, the region was returned to the French. They fortified the site and made it the capital of French Acadia from 1670-1674.

In 1674 the fort and settlement were attacked by a Dutch ship and destroyed. It was never rebuilt.

The site was excavated by University of Maine

archeology crews in the mid 1980s. A half dozen stone buildings were excavated. These included a chapel, enlisted men's barracks, entrance gate, forge, and the officer's quarters.

St. SAUVEUR (Hancock Co.)
class A-colonial village

At west end of Mt. Desert Island, 5.8 miles southwest of Somesville.

In June, 1613, Fathers Peter Biard and Ennemond Masse landed here and built homes and a fort for protection from the English. Three months later, English Captain Samuel Argall destroyed the small village, and captured Masse and 14 settlers. They were taken to sea and set adrift. (They drifted north and landed in Nova Scotia.) Biard was taken to Virginia, and that was the end of the colony.

Other ghost towns in Maine include...

AMHERST (Hancock Co.)
class Db-logging

At the junction of SH 9 and SH 181, 25 miles east of Bangor, this old logging boom town has faded to a 1990 population of 100. It once had a saw mill, grist mill, clapboard and shingle mills, and a large tannery.

DREW (Penobscot Co.)
class A-lumbering

An early 1900s logging community that had train service, a boarding house, general store, ice house, post office, two-room schoolhouse and the sawmill. When the last of the mills shut down after their 30 year run, the town was deserted. Today, nothing remains where this busy community once stood on the Mattawamkeag River, between Kingman and Wytopitlock, in the northeastern corner of the county.

EAGLE LAKE LOGGING CAMPS (Piscataquis Co.)
class B-logging camps

A cluster of old logging camps between Chamberlain Lake and Eagle Lake, in the northern portion of the county. This is a location that local research should provide exact locations for. The camps operated in the 1927-1933 period. Remains include a tramway, railroad grade, and other rubble.

For the researcher...

FOREST CITY (Washington Co...lumber town), LINDSEY TAVERN (York Co...wayside station), PARKER CAMP (Sagadahac Co...small island fishing village), PUNKINTOWN (York Co...an old site on York Pond), St. GEORGE (Sagadahoc Co...English colony dating to 1607).

New Hampshire

LIVERMORE (Grafton Co.)
class B-lumbering

Midway between Plymouth and Blair, just off I-93.

This sawmill town was established in 1876, and had a peak population of about 300. It was here that the former practice of clearcutting was modified by the Saunders family. They pioneered the selective cutting method, which helped to save the logging industry in the state.

Livermore declined after the mill burned in 1920. It was rebuilt, but in 1927 floods destroyed much of the railroad that supplied the town, and in 1928 the mills shut down for good, killing the village. In 1936, the townsite was sold to the forest service, and disincorporated in 1951. The last buildings burned in 1965.

COBURNVILLE (Strafford Co.)
class B-manufacturing

Along Hayes Brook, on the side of Birch Hill southeast of Coburn.

This small village was the site of the F.W. Coburn Knife Factory that was built in 1856. The knives were originally made for use in the shoe manufacturing business. The company also branched out into butcher knives. Coburn's were considered the finest knives made.

All that remains are the foundations of the plant, some outbuildings, and the remains of a dam on the creek.

SANDWICH NOTCH (Carroll Co.)
class B-agricultural

At the northwestern corner of the county, northwest of Center and North Sandwich.

In 1760, this small community was founded in a mountain meadow below the notch that bears its name. It grew slowly, and the rich farmlands invited growth. In 1850 the village was at its peak with a sawmill, three schools, a still, and a tavern among its businesses.

By 1910 the last person left, and the old community crumbled. Today nothing but foundation outlines and rubble remain under the everpresent greenery.

Other ghost towns in New Hampshire include...

DERRYFIELD (Rockingham Co.)
class C-rural village

This is an old town whose only remains are the occupied two story, white clapboard Gamble Hall, several miles southeast of Manchester.

ELLSWORTH (Grafton Co.)
class Da-lumbering

This small declining logging camp is located on a small road four miles northwest of West Campton, in the southern end of the White Mountain National Forest. In 1980 there were only 53 people, and as they move out, the US Forest Service tears down their houses.

SNACKITY (Strafford Co.)
class B-farming

Near Blue Job Mountain, between Strafford and Rochester, in the western part of the county.

All that remains of this late 1700s farming community are cellar holes and a cemetery. There are still a few occupied, but scattered homes. The town faded out in the early 1900s, and in 1956, the last large structure, the meetinghouse, was torn down and relocated to Concord, Massachusetts.

ZEALAND (Grafton Co.)
class A-lumbering

South of US 302, about six miles west of Bretton Woods. The Zealand River and Zealand Campground are just east and south of Twin Mountain. This is another old logging town that thrived in the late 1800s and early 1900s.

For the researcher...

HILL (Merrimack Co...town relocated in 1941), LEATHER CITY (Strafford Co...southwest of Rochester), QUINNTOWN Grafton Co... in 1830 had 15 houses & a number of sawmills). ROXBURY CENTER (Cheshire Co...old farming town), SUCCESS (Coos Co...1980 population of 2).

Vermont

CHIMNEY POINT TAVERN/FORT de PIEUX (Addison Co.)

class C (museum)-tavern
class B-French outpost

At the south end of Lake Champlain, where the Champlain Bridge crosses to New York. Just off SH 17, eight miles southwest of Addison.

Jacobus de Warm of Albany, New York, originally established an outpost here in 1690, but it was abandoned a few months later. Then in 1730 the French rebuilt it and named it Fort de Pieux. By 1759 it was deserted, and has since fallen into ruin. Cellar holes and rubble remain. Also at the site is the Chimney Point Tavern, an 18th Century tavern that is the interpretive center for the site.

FORT STE. ANNE (Grand Co.)

class B-French colonial outpost

On West Shore Road, three miles north of the village of Isle la Motte, on Isle La Motte (island), in the northwest corner of Lake Champlain.

This fort was built by the French under the command of Captain Pierre de la Motte in 1666 for protection against the Mohawk Indians. A small settlement was built up around the fort. The Mohawks destroyed the fort and settlement in 1670. Nothing much remains.

PLYMOUTH FIVE CORNERS (Windsor Co.)
class B-farming

Near Plymouth.

It was near this little agricultural village that Vermont's gold rush occurred. In 1855, Matthew Kennedy, a returning gold miner from California, panned for and found gold in Reading Pound Brook. It wasn't a lot, but despite his secrecy, Reading Pound, Broad and Buffalo Brooks were overrun with people looking for quick riches.

For four years the call of gold echoed through the wooded hills around Plymouth Five Corners, a small agricultural village. Placer claims were filed along Gold Brook, and the miners converged on the tiny community. As they arrived, the tiny hamlet grew, adding a couple hotels, and a wandering butcher. The hotels rented out rooms and provided liquid refreshment.

As 1860 faded and the nation's focus shifted to the increased tensions between the North and South, gold was forgotten, until 1880. A group of miners traced the gold in Buffalo Creek to a vein high on the slope above it, and the Rooks Mine began operation in 1882. By 1884 the Rooks Mine was big news in the area, as it was producing $50/ton ore.

But in 1887 the Rooks mine was bankrupt, and the gold rush was over. Today, the mine buildings are long gone, and little remains to mark the area where the village with two hotels was.

Other ghost towns in Vermont include...

GLASTENBURY (Bennington Co.)
class B-agricultural

All that remains of this old farming town on the Appalachian Trail, ten air miles ortheast of Bennington, are cellar holes and rubble. At one time there was a hotel, charcoal kilns, and a railroad line.

MOSQUITOVILLE (Caledonia Co.)
class B-agricultural

In a marshy area south of Harvey Lake, two miles south of West Barnet, about 15 miles southwest of St. Johnsbury. All that remains of this old farming community is overgrown cellar holes and rubble.

SOMERSET (Windham Co.)
class B-agricultural

South of Somerset Reservoir, 12 miles northwest of Wilmington. This is another abandoned farming hamlet full of overgrown cellar holes.

STRATTON (Windham Co.)
class B-agricultural

In the green Mountains, fourmiles west of West Wardsboro. Daniel Webster gave a speech here in front of 20,000 Vermonters during his 1840 election campaign. The location is nothing more than memories and overgrown cellar holes.

For the researcher...

AVERY'S GORE (Essex Co...disenfranchised in 1963), CALEDONIA SPRING HOUSE (Caledonia Co...resort), SLAB CITY (Caledonia Co...farming community), STRAFFORD

COPPER MINE (Orange Co...copper mine closed in 1858), VERSHIRE COPPER MINE (Orange Co...1880s copper mine).

Dust in the Wind

The South

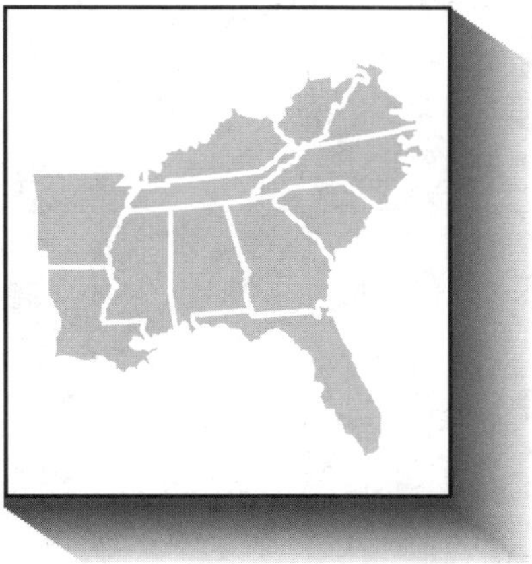

Western style ghost towns do not exist in the South. Of course that doesn't mean there are no ghost towns. In fact the truth is just the opposite. Especially along the Atlantic Coast. Like the northeastern states, this part of the country has over 400 years of settlement history. During that period, there have been thousands of locations that have been established, lived a few years then died out, long forgotten.

Crossroads taverns grew into crossroads settlements, then faded out as improved transportation methods rendered them obsolete. Ferry crossings were replaced by bridges. Fishing villages and beachfront resorts were destroyed by hurricanes. Cotton plantations located around small communities disappeared as the old South was destroyed by war. Gold mining camps sprouted through the Piedmont region were weakened and killed by the siren call of gold across the continent in California. Coal mining towns faded out as diesel fuel replaced coal as the motive power for trains, and as environmental concerns lessened our dependence on the burnable black rock. Military coastal defense forts have been abandoned as seaborne threats from England, France and Spain have evaporated.

Whether a 1600s English colony, or a 1900s logging camp, the Southern states have ghost towns. Again like in the northeast, many of the remaining sites with standing buildings have been absorbed into State or National historic sites/parks, and may have an admission fee. Hidden in the backwoods and sideroads of the south are thousands of old sites that await a patient researcher to reveal the sites to them.

Chapter Sixteen

Kentucky

BLUE HERON (McCreary Co.)
class C/F (restored-NRA)-coal mining

On SH 742, nine miles southwest of Stearns at the west end of Mine 18 Road.

This company coal mining camp was supported by Mine 18. It employed 300 miners, and was carved into the side of a mountain overlooking the Big South Fork of the Cumberland River. The camp consisted of wooden homes, a store, church and school. The buildings have been restored and the site is operated as a concession in the Big South Fork National River and Recreation Area.

COLUMBUS (Hickman Co.)
class A-rural community

Along the Mississippi River, at the junction of SH 58 and SH 123, nine miles northwest of Clinton.

In 1814, Washington, D.C. burned, and a number of industrious individuals platted the town of Columbus along the Mississippi and put in a bid to relocate the nation's capital. That bid failed, but the small community still grew, but slowly.

The town was subjected to periodic flooding, and in 1927 it relocated east of the original site. Today

Columbus is a small town of 252 people, and the original site is long forgotten.

FORT HEIMAN (Calloway Co.)
class B-military post

Overlooking the Tennessee River, about six miles southeast of New Concord.

In 1862, this was a defensive fort in process of being built by Confederate forces. When Fort Henry across the Tennessee River in Tennessee was overwhelmed and shelled by seven Union gunships under the leadership of General Ulysses S. Grant, and destroyed, the fort was abandoned. Since Fort Heiman was incomplete, an opening was forced through the Rebel line.

Fort Heiman was then occupied by Union troops for a year or so. They completed the earthworks, and used its strategic location to hold the region. In 1864, the Union troops moved out, and Confederate General Nathan Bedford Forrest moved in with a small regiment of Confederate troops. The unit installed cannons and disrupted Union shipping on the river below by sinking and capturing ships.

After the war ended, the fort fell into disuse and the forest eventually reclaimed it.

Other ghost towns in Kentucky include...

BEAVER IRON FURNACE/SCRANTON (Menifee Co.)
class B/Db-iron furnace

On SH 1274, eight miles northwest of Frenchburg at Scranton. The iron furnace was established in 1819 in the small community of Scranton, which had a 1990 population of 30. Ruins of the furnace remain.

CLINTON IRON FURNACE (Boyd Co.)
class C-iron furnace

On US 60 at junction with SH 538. It was originally built by the Poage brothers in 1833.

PRINCESS FURNACE (Boyd Co.)
class C-iron furnace

Nine miles southwest of Ashland, on SH 5 at the town of Princess (1990 pop of 400). The furnace was built by John Means and dates to 1864.

For the researcher...

BUFFALO FURNACE (Greenup Co...1870s iron furnace), CEDAR BLUFF (Caldwell Co...1990 population of 20), GOLDEN POND (Trigg Co...1990 pop of 5), RUCKERVILLE (Clark Co... 1990 population 25), YOCUM (Morgan Co...1990 pop 10).

Tennessee

AMIS (Hawkins Co.)
class C-milling/way station

On east side of Rogersville, along Big Creek.

Thomas Amis (A-MEE) established a small stage stop and store along an old stage route. The small community that grew up around Thomas Amis' store consisted of a water powered grist mill with a furniture manufacturing shop on the second floor, a tannery/saddle & harness shop, general store/post office, blacksmith shop, stage station/ tavern, and a log fort to protect the settlers from local Indians.

By 1970, most of the buildings were gone.

FORT DONELSON (Stewart Co.)

class C/F (restored)-National Battlefield

Just west of Dover, which is on the Cumberland River and US 79, 37 miles west of Clarksville.

Union General Ulysses S. Grant led a flotilla of gunboats against Fort Henry in February, 1862. Most of the Confederate troops that occupied that fort retreated to Fort Donelson (to the east), while the few that remained there and at Fort Heiman, KY. surrendered to Grant and his 15,000 man army. This was the Union's first major battle victory in the South and marked the turning point in the war.

At Fort Donelson the Union troops nearly overran the Confederates on February 13. Grant's army grew to 27,000, and after about 2700 rebel soldiers tried to escape, General Simon Buckner surrendered his force of 13,000 to Grant on February 16.

The National Battlefield park contains the restored hotel where Buckner surrendered, earthworks, the fort's cannon batteries, and a national cemetery.

RUGBY (Morgan Co.)

class Da/F (restored-$)-utopian colony

On SH 52 at northern point of county, 20 miles southeast of Jamestown.

On October 5, 1880, the English social reformer and writer Thomas Hughes started a cooperative, class-free colony called Rugby. The colonists were mostly English "gentlemen" whose family status allowed only professions in law, medicine or the clergy. He wanted his colonists to pursue any line of work they deemed fit to pursue.

In 1881 a typhoid epidemic swept through the new colony, staggering, but not killing it. The colony continued to grow slowly, and in 1884 it had 450 people and 65 buildings. That year the Tabard Inn burned to the ground.

Coupled with mismanagement and bad weather the colony faded rapidly and disbanded.

After the colony folded, a small town continued at the site, and even today there is a small resident population of 70 or so that watches over the historic old colony. Of the original buildings, only the bookstore, commissary, church, 7000 volume library, school, Hughes' home, and 11 other buildings have been restored to period splendor, and are open to the public.

Other ghost towns in Tennessee include...

APPLETON (Lawrence Co.)
class C-agricultural

In 1880 Appleton was founded along west fork of Sugar Creek in the far southeast corner of the county, east of Bonnertown. The 1880 census showed 60 people there. In 1950 there were 200, and today no population figures are available.

FORT LOUDOUN (Monroe Co.)
class C/F (restored)-military post

The first British-built fort west of the Appalachian Mountains sits just off US 411, a mile east of Vonore, just south of the bridge over the Little Tennessee River. It was built in 1756 to protect British interests from the French. The British allied with the Cherokee Indians, but after they mistreated them, the Cherokees burned the fort in 1760, killing over 20 soldiers. The fort has been restored.

For the researcher...

CHASKA (Campbell Co...abandoned coal mining camp), COLLIERVILLE (Shelby Co...original site founded in 1820, moved to railroad), GALBREATH

SPRINGS (Hawkins Co...old resort), NEWSOM'S STATION (Davidson Co...1862 mill and major stopping point).

West Virginia

GARY (McDowell Co.)
class Db-coal mining

On SH 103, six miles south of Welch.

In 1970, this once prosperous coal mining town had a population of 2712 people, and nestled along the Tug River in the south tip of the state. In July, 1986, US Steel closed its mine, and the population dropped to 1600.

A year later downtown buildings such as the Miner's Union Hall, bank, beauty shop, boarding houses, clothing stores, recreation center, several restaurants, and theatre have all closed. In 1987 the grocery, a gas station, car wash and pool hall were still open, but the future looked real bleak.

Coal mining began in the Tug River valley in 1895, and at one time there were many old coal mining camps. During the 1940s it is claimed that 15,000 people lived in Gary and the neighboring 15 unnamed coal camps. Gary and the smaller camps were company towns, but in the 1950s, many of the homes were sold to the people, and many torn down as they were vacated. Each of these small camps were self sufficient, and as the mines closed so did the theaters, stores and gas stations.

In 1970 Gary incorporated, but in the 1990s it is in trouble. It had a population of 1355 in 1990.

ROWLESBURG (Preston Co.)
class Db-mountain town

On SH 72, just two miles north of US 50, 15 miles south of Kingwood.

In early November, 1985, this town of 1006 was badly flooded by the Cheat River. Over half of its 341 homes were damaged or washed away. By 1990 only 468 people remained.

Other ghost towns in West Virginia include...

CASS (Pocahontas Co.)
class Db-lumbering

In the center of the county, 16 air miles northeast of Marlinton, Cass was a major lumbering center in the early 1900s. It has faded to a small town of about 150 people. The West Virginia Pulp and Paper General Store was claimed to have been the largest company store in the world. Today, the Cass Country Store occupies the old building.

HENRY CLAY IRON FURNACE (Preston Co.)
class B-iron furnace

An iron furnace was built at or near Bruceton Mills, east of Morgantown, in the 1830s. The stone structure was soon surrounded by a small village. The furnaces's smoke stack is square and stands 30 feet tall. It closed after only a dozen years of shipping pig iron.

For the researcher...

ADVENT (Jackson Co...1990 population of 50), FORT NEALLY (Berkeley Co...Colonial fort dating back to 1756), JACKO INN (Doddridge Co...an old tavern/wayside stop that has several treasure legends attached to it),

MIRACLE RUN (Monongalla Co...20 people lived here in 1990), WILDCAT (Lewis Co...15 people in 1980).

Chapter Seventeen

North Carolina

FORT RALEIGH/ROANOKE COLONY (Dare Co.)
class B (NHS)-British colony

On Pierce Street, a quarter mile north of US 64, just east of the William Umstead Bridge on the north end of Roanoke Island, three miles north of Manteo.

Under the leadership of Sir Richard Grenville and Ralph Lane, 108 colonists from England landed near here in late June, 1585, founding England's first colony in the New World. Financed by Sir Walter Raleigh (Grenville's cousin), who remained safely back at home, the colonists erected a large earth bulwark for protection against the possibility of attack by the Spanish.

As it was too late in the year to plant new crops, Grenville returned to England for provisions, planning on returning before winter. Friction between the local Indians and the intruders created ill-will, and the two factions ended up trying to decimate each other.

By Easter of 1586, Grenville still hadn't returned, and things were so intolerable, that when Sir Francis Drake stopped by the colony offering one of his ships for the colonists to return to England, they accepted his offer.

Two days later a supply ship arrived at the abandoned colony. The sailors searched in vain for the missing colonists, and headed back to England. Within two weeks, Grenville and his ships arrived and also searched for the missing colonists, not knowing they had already left. 15 men remained behind with two years of supplies, while Grenville headed back to England to round up more settlers.

Reconstructed earth bulwalks at the Roanoke Colony site, NC

On July 22, 1587, he returned with 150 people, finding an abandoned colony. Grenville had planned to pick up his 15 men and relocate in the Chesapeake Bay area. Again it was too late in the year to grow enough crops to last the winter, so a decision had to be made...move north or stay here through the winter. They decided to stay and move north in the Spring.

A month later the new governor, John White organized a provisioning trip to England so they could have enough supplies to last the winter. When White arrived in England his ship was confiscated for war service in a threatened war with Spain. He went to Sir Walter Raleigh to try and obtain a small supply ship so he could immediately return with provisions for his people.

Three years later, on August 12, 1590, he returned to an abandoned colony. The houses had been destroyed, and there was no sign of the people except a mysterious word carved into a post..."CROATOAN".

The fate of all three sets of colonists has never been determined.

Between 1936 and 1948, the site of the old fort and colony was discovered, and archaeological excavations made. In 1950 the earthworks were reconstructed, and this is the centerpiece of the National Historic Park that is now at the site.

REED GOLD MINE (Cabarrus Co.)

class C/F (museum/tours)-gold mining

1.6 miles southwest of Georgetown, which is on SH 200, 14.4 miles southeast of Concord.

12-year-old Conrad Reed skipped church and played in Little Meadow Creek on a Sunday morning in 1799. He dragged home a heavy, yellow, brick-sized rock, which was used as a doorstop until 1802 when a Fayetteville jeweler identified it as a large gold nugget. He bought it from John Reed for $3.50. After the value was determined, Reed demanded another $1000, which he got.

Reed and his brother-in-law Frederick Kiser searched for and found more gold on the farm's streams. Neighboring farmers took notice and searched their own land. By the 1820s, the entire Piedmont area from Virginia south through northeastern Alabama became a hotbed of mining.

The streams on the Reed farm were worked by

Headframe at the Reed Gold Mine, NC

family members and slaves, and by 1829 they had found about $200,000 in gold by placer mining alone. In 1831 the family began hardrock mining, which enlarged the operations.

When Reed died in 1845, his will said the mine was to be sold and the money divided among his heirs. Several relatives pooled money buying out the others, but in 1852 they sold out to a New York company. Two years later America's first major gold mine was sold at auction.

In the 1890s, the Kelly family from Springfield, Ohio (Kelly Tire Co.) purchased the long idle mine and began development. In 1896, a 23 pound nugget was discovered in one of the tunnels, but that wasn't enough to sustain the old mine, and in 1912 it closed. The Kelly family remained owners until 1971 when they sold to the state of North Carolina. The state repaired the mine, installed a museum and opened it for visitors on April 23, 1977.

Underground at the Reed Gold Mine, NC

Other ghost towns in North Carolina include...

BRUNSWICK TOWN (Brunswick Co.)
class B (SHS)-Colonial seaport

On the west side of Cape Fear River, 19 miles south of Wilmington. This busy colonial seaport was founded around 1725, and burned by British troops in 1776. Archaeologists have uncovered about 60 foundations. The site has a museum and interpretive center for visitors.

CATALOOCHEE (Haywood Co.)
class C-agricultural

Located in Cataloochee Valley, at the eastern end of Smoky Mountain National Park. Cataloochee dates back to 1814. In the 1930s Smoky Mountains National Park was formed, and it absorbed Cataloochee. Since the town was now part of the National Park, residents couldn't make any modifications or improvements to their homes or businesses. By 1950 the community was abandoned, and most of the buildings were torn down by the National Park Service. Some still remain.

FORT LANDING (Tyrrell Co.)
class C-ferry landing

Eight miles north of US 64. The turnoff is six miles west of the Alligator River Bridge. This old ferry landing is hidden in the trees. Remains include a ferry landing, log store building and an occupied mobile home of fairly recent vintage.

GOLD HILL (Rowan Co.)
class Db-mining

On US 52, 25 miles northeast of Concord. A real wild, rip-snorting gold boom town, years before the California

Downtown Fort Landing, NC

Gold Rush was even heard of. The Gold Hill Mine was 425' deep and the miners worked by candle light. The 1848 discovery of gold in California crippled the mines, but it took the Civil War to kill them. Today the town is just another faceless one street community of 300 people.

For the researcher...

ATLANTIC (Carteret Co., original site destroyed by hurricane in 1775), BETHABARA (Forsyth Co...1st Moravian colony in the state), FORT FISHER (New Hanover Co...Civil War era fort), PARKEWOOD (Moore Co...only rubble remains of this old milling town), VALE (Lincoln Co...1990 population of 50).

Virginia

APPOMATTOX COURT HOUSE (Appomattox Co.)
class C/F (NHP-$)-county seat

On SH 24, three miles northeast of the town of Appomattox.

Peaceful Appomattox Court House village, VA

In 1819, the Clover Hill Tavern opened on the Richmond-Lynchburg Road. It became a popular stopping point and as the inn grew, farmhouses grew up around it. In 1845 when Appomattox County was established the small but growing village obtained county seat honors.

Now that its future seemed secure, a post office was

The Civil War ended in the parlor of this house.
Appomattox Court House, VA

established, and the courthouse was built along with law offices and other assorted government related businesses. Clover Hill changed its name to Appomattox Court House, and through the 1850s the village of 150 people prospered.

On Palm Sunday, 1865, fate and the rapidly approaching end of the Civil War intervened. Outside of town the armies of Generals Robert E. Lee and Ulysses S. Grant faced off. The Generals arranged a meeting to be held in town so Lee could formally surrender his troops to Grant, ending the Civil War. At that time the prosperous little town consisted of the courthouse, two blacksmith shops, county jail, law offices, two stables, three stores, the tavern, and a number of homes.

Since the courthouse was closed on Sundays, Lee and Grant searched the town for a suitable site, settling on the parlor of the three-story brick home of Wilmer McLean.

The war ended, and prosperity disappeared. The nearby railroad station of Appomattox Station grew, pulling trade and population from the old town. In 1892 the courthouse burned, so the county seat was transferred to Appomattox Station, which dropped the "station" from its name.

As time went on, old Appomattox Court House village was abandoned and the buildings either burned, were razed or were moved. On June 18, 1930 the site was purchased by the federal government and on August 3, 1935, plans for restoration of Appomattox Court House village became a reality. The National Historic Park was born, and on April 6, 1954 the park opened with the two dozen or so buildings restored to how they looked when the truce was signed.

JAMESTOWN (James River Co.)
class B (NHS-$)-English colony

On the north bank of the James River, 10.8 miles southwest of Williamsburg.

On May 13, 1607, three small ships from England landed on the shore of the James River. Within five days a colony had been started, and from that flimsy start Jamestown developed as England's second oldest colony in the New World (Roanoke, NC. was the first). By September, 1609, nearly 500 settlers were at the colony. Captain John Smith returned to England ostensibly to bring more provisions and settlers. He never returned, but the ships that did next May found only 60 people remaining. The colony was saved and it remained England's Colonial capital until 1699 when Williamsburg grabbed that title, leaving the filthy swampy site of Jamestown to those that wanted to remain.

Reconstructed foundations at Jamestown, VA

Few did, and the site quickly fell into ruin.

Since 1934, the site has been a part of Colonial National Historic Park. The foundations and tumbled down walls of a number of buildings have been excavated. A private tourist attraction replica of the original Jamestown (Jamestown Settlement) is next door.

WILDERNESS TAVERN (Spotsylvania Co.)
class B-tavern/way station

On SH 3 at the junction with SH 20, 12 miles northwest of Fredericksburg.

The Wilderness Tavern was a busy cross roads complex with a tavern, blacksmith shop, tailor, and general store that catered to travelers on the old Fredericksburg-Orange Turnpike. On May 2, 1863 the community became a huge field hospital to care for the Confederate forces

Remains of the last building at Wilderness Tavern, VA

that were wounded during the Battle of Chancellorsville. Over 3000 men were treated in the existing buildings and a huge assortment of tents. One of the patients was Lt. General Stonewall Jackson, who had his left arm amputated here in the makeshift field hospital. He died a week later.

All but one of the buildings were eventually destroyed by the war, and that one burned in 1978, leaving only fallen walls and a stone chimney.

Other ghost towns in Virginia include...

GOLD HILL (Buckingham Co.)
class Da-gold mining

This old gold mining community is a tiny village today with a population of 90. It sits along US 15, eight miles northeast of Dillwyn, a skeleton of the booming gold mining center it once was. All that remains are an abandoned store, active gas station/store, laundry, and a few houses.

What's left of Gold Hill, VA

GOLDVEIN (Fauquier Co.)
class Db-gold mining

This tiny town of 35 is the nearest town to the Franklin Mine, which was in operation from 1837-1936. Foundations and ruins remain of the old mine. Another local mine was the Liberty Mine, which began in March, 1834. Many other mines dot the gold mining region around Goldvein, which is on US 17, 18 miles northwest of Fredericksburg.

MITCHIE TAVERN (Albemarle Co.)
class C/F (restored-$)-tavern/wayside stop

On SH 53, a mile and a half south of I-64 at EXIT

124, just east of Charlottesville. This historic old tavern was originally opened around 1784, and operated until 1927, when it was moved to its present location.

For the researcher...

BRENT TOWN (Fauquier Co...dates back to 1688), DUNKARD BOTTOM (Pulaski Co...a 1750s hamlet), GERMANNA (Orange Co...German colony dating to 1714), GRASTY TRACT MINE Orange Co...near the semi-ghost of Mine Run), MOUNT AIRY (Wythe Co...a 1779s village).

Gary Speck

Chapter Eighteen

Alabama

CAHABA (Dallas Co.)

class B-former state capital

At end of SH 2, 3.5 miles southeast of SH 22, at a point nine miles southwest of Selma.

When Alabama was established as a state in 1819, the search for an ideal location to establish a capital city lead to the confluence of the Cahaba and Alabama Rivers The centerpiece of the new city was the two story capital building, which opened in 1820. That year saw a bank, churches, hotels, two newspapers, school, and at least one tavern. Cahaba also served as the county seat. As the town continued to build, a flood in April of 1825 nearly washed it away.

Realizing that the site was susceptible to flooding, the state legislature voted to move the capital, and in 1826 it was relocated to Tuscaloosa. Despite the flood, the town's citizens began to rebuild the former capital city. They felt it still had a promising future as a major riverport on the Alabama. The town soon had several thousand people. In 1833 another flood heavily damaged the town, but again the citizens bounced back and rebuilt better than ever, and by 1850, 5000 people lived there.

In 1864, a 2000 man prisoner of war camp was

located here. Neither Cahaba or the POW camp lasted much longer as Union troops routed protecting Confederate troops, and Cahaba's townsfolk buried their wealth, shuttered their windows and waited for the human storm to approach. They watched nearby Selma being reduced to a smoking ember, but before Union troops could arrive in Cahaba, a third flood destroyed the city.

That was it.

The citizens packed up and left, abandoning the town. The county seat was transferred to Selma, and Cahaba was a memory.

Today it is a rubbled site, and part of an state owned Archeologic Interpretive Park.

DAUPHIN/FORT GAINES (Mobile Co.)
class A-French settlement/fort
class C ($)-American military post

On Dauphin Island, which is on the west side of the mouth of Mobile Bay.

Sometime between 1699 and 1702 Jean Baptiste le Moyne established a small settlement on the east tip of Massacre Island, called that because of the large number of human bones found on the shore. In 1711 the settlement was relocated to the mainland, and the island was renamed Dauphin Island. (Some sources claim this was in 1717.) During the Civil War, Fort Gaines, also on the east tip of the island was one of the major coastal defense forts protecting Mobile from Union attack. It was built on the site of the French fort in 1861, and is a huge brick structure. The fort was remodeled in 1898, and remained active until 1946.

It is open for visitors.

FORT MORGAN (Baldwin Co.)
class C (NR-$)-military post

On the east side of the mouth of Mobile Bay, at the west tip of the peninsula west of Gulf Shores.

In 1812 Fort Bowyer was built, but it was destroyed by storms in 1819. Construction on Fort Morgan began around 1819 (one source claims 1818, another 1833), and was completed in 1834. Like Fort Gaines, this was one of the coastal forts protecting Mobile from Union attack. On August 23, 1864, the garrison surrendered after the two-week long Battle of Mobile Bay ended.

During the Spanish American War, and both world wars, it was an active military post, closing in 1945. It is now state owned.

TANNEHILL IRON WORKS (Jefferson Co.)
class C/F (restored-NR-$)-iron forge

Two miles east of I-20/59 at EXIT 100, southwest of Birmingham.

In 1829, the operation began as a small forge, and in 1855 the first charcoal powered blast furnace was built. In 1863 two more furnaces were added, and Tannehill became a major supplier of shot and other material for Confederate forces. The charcoal furnaces consumed 3000 acres of hardwood forests, pumping out 20 tons of iron daily.

On March 31, 1865 Major General James Wilson and 14,000 Union troops marched into the heart of Alabama's iron country to rip out the heart of the Confederate industrial strength. A detachment led by Captain William A. Sutherland destroyed the entire Tannehill operation, including a grist mill, tannery, and quarters for the 600 slaves that were "employed" at the furnaces.

In 1969, the site became a State Park, which contains a restored furnace. Ruins of the other two furnaces are undergoing restoration. There is also an operating grist mill (1867-1931) and cotton gin, museum and 30 old buildings relocated from all over the state.

Other ghost towns in Alabama include...

ARBACOOCHE MINE (Cleburne Co.)
class B-gold mining

Eight miles south of Helfin.

Large gold nuggets were found in 1832, and the excitement was enough to enable a mining camp to expand to a population reported to be 2500. When gold was discovered in California, the majority of the miners left. The mines and town struggled through the last half of the 1800s, and in 1900 the mine closed, killing the town.

CORNWALL FURNACE (Cherokee Co.)
class C (NHS)-iron forge

On SH 9, two miles east of Cedar Bluff.

This water powered, cold-blast furnace was built in 1862 by the Noble brothers of Georgia. The furnace was a major ironwork during the Civil War. In 1972 it was made a National Historic Site.

WALDO (Talladega Co.)
class Db-gold mining

On SH 77, five miles southeast of Talladega.

In the 1830s, Waldo was the center for hardrock mining. The mines included the Gold Log (operated until 1940), May Virginia Mine (which had a small mining camp and a 100 room hotel next to the mine.), and the Riddles Mine ($20-150 per ton ore in the 1930s). With a 1990 population of 309, Waldo is a sleepy semi-ghost that has faded from its glory days.

For the researcher...

ALABAMA WHITE SULPHUR SPRINGS (DeKalb Co...late 1800s & early 1900s resort), BRIERFIELD (Bibb Co....population decrease from 2040 in 1938, to 150 in

1990), MASSILON (Dallas Co...population dropped from 70 in 1938 to 0 in 1980), PIPER (Bibb Co...had a 1938 population of 2043, & isn't listed in current atlases), YOLANDE (Tuscaloosa Co..1938 population of 1030, & 1990 population of 0).

Arkansas

ARKANSAS POST (Arkansas Co.)
class B (NHP)-riverport

On SH 169, a mile east of US 165 four miles north of its crossing of the Arkansas River.

In 1686, Henri de Tonti, established a trading post along the north side of the Arkansas River, but in 1689 it fell into disuse until the Spaniards showed interest in the area. In 1762, France ceded the land to Spain, and the Spanish established a fort here called Fort St. Charles III. Around 1800 France took over again, then in 1803, the Louisiana Purchase turned the region over to American control. The site grew, and it became a busy steamboat landing, riverport, and territorial capital.

Arkansas Post eventually reached a population of 3500, had many homes, a bank, brick factory, and race track as well as other businesses. In the late 1800s, after the railroads reached the area, the steamboat trade decreased, and the town faded.

Today all that remains is rubble and filled in cellars.

CADRON (Faulkner Co.)
class A-steamboat port

At the confluence of Cadron Creek with the Arkansas River, west of Conway.

A quiet town of a half dozen homes and a log tavern with a sawmill to keep the folks occupied. Cadron was founded in 1814 by a trapper named John Standlee. In 1820, Cadron and Little Rock contested for the Pulaski County seat as well as territorial capitol, and Cadron lost. When the steamboat era arrived just before the Civil War the community boomed and became a bustling riverport. It faded as the steamship era ended, and today is almost forgotten.

CHAMPAGNOLLE LANDING (Union Co.)
class B-riverport

On the Ouachita River, several miles southeast of Calion, which is on US 167.

One of the oldest towns in southern Arkansas, this onetime riverport has changed names several times. It was first called Scarborough Landing and was a busy steamboat port along the Ouachita River. In 1840, when the small town obtained the Union County seat honors, it was renamed Union Courthouse.

In 1844 the county seat was moved to El Dorado, and the town faded. As late as the 1960s there were still a number of abandoned buildings still standing.

WITTSBURG (Cross Co.)
class Da-riverport

Two miles from Levesque, on the St. Francis River.

In 1739, the French governor of Louisiana, Bienville, built a fort along the St. Francis River. In 1803 with the region transferring to American hands, the location was called Strong's Point, and from 1862-1868 was the county seat of Cross County.

Towards the 1870s, as steamboat trade dwindled, the town faded. In 1886 the county seat was relocated to Vanndale. Today not much remains except a spread out rural community. As late as 1979 the old school still stood, along with a store and houses.

Other ghost towns in Arkansas include...

BROWNSVILLE (Lonoke Co.)
class B-former county seat

Located 25 miles east of Little Rock and three miles northeast of Lonoke, this site was established in 1846. It was the original county seat of Prairie County before Lonoke County was established. During the Civil War, Union Troops secured the area and left the town. Looters and vandals moved in and stripped it of all valuables, then burned it. Only a few homes mark the site.

DAVIDSONVILLE (Randolph Co.)
class B-state park

On SH 166, at the Black River, nine miles south of US 62 at a point two miles west of Pocahontas.

Davidsonville was established as early as 1801. It had a blacksmith shop, church, dry goods shops, hardware store, jewelry shop, saloons and the first post office, courthouse and land office in the state. It died in 1828 or 1829 when a ship landed and a virulent epidemic swept through town.

MARIANNA (1st site) (Lee Co.)
class B-riverport

On the L'Anguille River, 1.5 miles west from the present town. The old site at one time was the head of navigation on the L'Anguille River.

ROME (Arkansas Co.
class B-suburb of Arkansas Post

On a hill five miles from the present site of Arkansas Post. In the early 1800s, this hill town flourished, but when land titles were muddled, the town faded, and the people moved to Arkansas Post.

For the researcher...

COLUMBIA (Chicot Co...riverport and county seat), GRAYSONIA (Montgomery Co...lumber town active from 1906-1926), LEWISBURG (Conway Co...riverport with 1200 people), RONDO (Miller Co...mid 1800s town that has faded badly), TROTT'S STAND (Benton Co...onetime important stage stop).

Louisiana

FORT JACKSON (Plaquemines Parish)

class C (NHL, NR)-military post

On SH 23 and the west bank of the Mississippi River, 2.5 miles east of Triumph.

This American military fort was built in 1792, was strengthened and enlarged in 1815, and again in 1861 by the Confederate Army. It is a large, star-shaped brick fort with a surrounding moat. It served to protect New Orleans, but on April 18, 1862, Admiral Farragut and his fleet of 43 boats, battled the fort for a week. New Orleans fell, the fort surrendered, and his forces occupied them.

LOS ADAES (Natchitoches Parish)

class B (SHP-$)-Spanish fort/village

Just off SH 6, two miles northeast of Robeline.

This Spanish mission, fort (presidio) and village was

established in 1717 as the mission San Miguel de los Adaes. It was the only Spanish mission established in Louisiana, and was destroyed by the French in 1721. The Spaniards rebuilt the mission, protecting it with a fortified presidio next to the old site. A small village grew up beside it, and Los Adaes became the capital of the Texas frontier until 1773. Only rubble remains, but the site is a state historic park.

NEWLLANO (Vernon Parish)

class C-socialist colony

On US 171, two miles south of Leesville, and 51 miles southwest of Alexandria.

In the western reaches of Southern California's Mojave Desert, a socialistic colony called Llano del Rio was on its last legs (See chapter 2). Job Harriman, founder of that colony, heard about an abandoned lumber town in Louisiana. In October, 1917, he went to Louisiana, liked what he saw, and purchased the company town of Stables along with 20,000 acres of land from the Gulf Lumber Company.

Most of the California colonists packed up and headed east, and by the end of the year, Newllano was in business. Somewhere between 65 and 600 people made the move. A group of 25 families from east Texas also joined them.

By the early 1930s, the colony's population stabilized at about 400. 75 buildings were spread over a 60 acre site, which included a hospital, hotel, print shop, shoe shop, theatre, and many other trades and businesses. In 1935, a decade after Harriman died, the colony was wracked by litigation and internal conflict. In 1938 the colony fell into receivership, officially ending the colony. For the next decade members tried in vain to get the courts to reverse the decision. The small town of New Llano has absorbed the old site.

Other ghost towns in Louisiana include...

CAMINADA (Jefferson Parish)

class A-seaport

A thriving seaport town on the mainland side of Caminada Bay that was destroyed in an 1893 hurricane. It never recovered, and today the barren site is difficult to find.

FORT de la BOULAYE (Plaquemines Parish)

class B (NHL, NR)-French military post

On SH 39, a mile north of Phoenix. Also known as Fort Iberville, this fort was built in 1700 on the east bank of the Mississippi River. It was a 28' square blockhouse with a half dozen cannons. Its strategic location helped the French hold this part of the river and thus the state. In 1704 or so, it was abandoned.

GERMANTOWN (Webster Parish)

class C/F (restored-$)-German commune

On CR 114, seven miles northeast of Minden, this old German socialist-utopian colony was founded in 1835 and lasted for 37 years. Three original buildings remain, and other buildings have been re-created.

For the researcher...

CRANE'S FORGE (Assumtion Parish...iron forge town), GALVEZTOWN (Livingston Parish...fortified Spanish town), LINCEUM (Grant Parish...sawmill town), NIBLETT'S BLUFF (Calcasieu Parish...formerly busy riverport), SELMA (Grant Parish...late 1800s sawmill town.)

Mississippi

BAY SPRINGS (Tishomingo Co.)
class B-milling town

On SH 4 and the west side of Mack's Creek, five miles west of Dennis.

This 1880s milling town consisted of a cotton gin, corn mill, gambling halls, hotel and a couple of stores. A lost treasure legend is connected with the town. The son of one of the storekeepers is said to have buried a jar of gold coins.

FORT MASSACHUSETTS (Harrison Co.)
class C-military post

On Ship Island, 10 miles offshore from Gulfport.

Access to this historic 1859 era masonry coastal defense fort is by boat from Gulfport ($). It was under construction when the Civil War broke out. It was destroyed, and the Confederates rebuilt it. In September 1861 Union troops reoccupied the fort after wresting it from the rebels. It was used to hold war "detainees."

PANOLA (Panola Co.)
class C-riverport/county seat

An old riverport and former county seat along the Tallahatchie River near Batesville. When the railroad passed through, it bypassed the town. Panola relocated to the railroad, changing names to Batesville. One of the vacant buildings left behind was the brick courthouse, which was turned into a private home.

PRAIRIE MOUNT (Chickasaw Co.)
class B-rural community

Located six miles north of Okolona, which is on US 45A, 21 miles south of Tupelo. It originally was a stage coach stop, but when the railroad promised to pass through the region, it would miss the old town by a few miles, so in 1848 it moved to the railroad and renamed itself Okolona.

WHITE HORSE TAVERN (Adams Co.)
class A-roadside inn

At the junction of US 61 and the Old Woodville Road, several miles south of Natchez. This was an old travelers stop/tavern that has disappeared.

WINBORN (Benton Co.)
class Da-iron forge

On US 78, 15 miles southeast of Holly Springs.

In 1912 an iron foundry and its supporting town was established here, at the site of the only iron producing mine in Mississippi. Three years later the foundry closed, and the town faded. In 1990 it still had a population of 50.

For the researcher...

ANTIOCH (Prentiss Co...a large town that disappeared after the Civil War), AUGUSTA (Perry Co...original site across the Leaf River from New Augusta), LOGTOWN (Hancock Co...townsite near NASA Test Site), Mt. LOCUST INN (Adams Co...the last remaining Natchez Trace inn), PIAVE (Greene Co...former 1920s company lumber town).

Chapter Nineteen

Florida

CEDAR KEY (Levy Co.)
class E-port/lumber

At west end of SH 24, on West Coast of state, just off shore 54 miles southwest of Gainesville.

Was a major Gulf Coast seaport and one of the largest cities in the state in the early 1800s. In the early 1860s a fort was located here. Cedar Key was a major shipping point during the Civil War, when blockade runners ran cotton, timber and other goods from the port to bring in much needed capital. In 1862 Union forces captured the island, and it remained in Union hands until the war ended.

After the War, the port became a major timber, fishing and ship building center. Then in 1896 a hurricane ripped the town, and it never regained its status. Today the historic old town of Cedar Key is a quiet fishing town and resort with a 1990 population of 668 people, which is still way below what it was in the 1800s.

FORT JEFFERSON (Monroe Co.)
class C (NM)-military post

On Dry Tortugas Island, at the far western tip of the Florida Keys, 70 miles west of Key West.

Accessible by boat or seaplane ($) from Key West.

This historic post was the largest of the coastal defense forts on the east coast. Construction of the massive hexagonal brick fort began in 1846, and it almost covers the entire island. It was designed to garrison 1500 soldiers and its 50' high walls had three levels of firing platforms that would hold 450 cannons.

In January 1861, the as yet uncompleted and unarmed fort was occupied by armed Union troops to keep the fort from falling into Rebel hands. In 1865, after the war ended, the fort was not needed, so it was turned into a prison, housing a total of 2400 inmates. It was abandoned after an 1874 hurricane damaged it.

St. JOSEPH (Gulf Co.)
class A-seaport

On St. Joseph's Bay, just south of Port St. Joe, southeast of Panama City.

In the early 1800s, St. Joseph with a population of 6000 or so was the largest town in Florida, and was the site of the state's first Constitutional Convention. The busy seaport died an unusual death in 1841 when a ship carrying some victims of Yellow Fever docked. The disease spread rapidly, killing upwards of 75% of the town's population.

Those who survived the plague fled, leaving the town to the whims of nature, which rapidly took care of it by burying it with sand kicked up by high surf generated from a hurricane. The site is marked by a historical marker.

Other ghost towns in Florida include...

BULLOWVILLE (Flagler Co.)
class B-sugar plantation town

On CR 2001, nine miles southeast Bunnell. The ruins

of the sugar mill and plantation manor remain of what was once a large plantation with supporting worker's village. It was destroyed by Seminole Indians in 1836.

INDIAN KEY (Monroe Co.)
class B-early settlement

Southwest of Islamorada, a little less than a mile southeast of Lower Matecumbe Key. Tours leave from mile post 78.5 ($). The small island was settled originally by Captain Jacob Housman in the early 1830s, then followed by Botanist Dr. Henry Perrine and his family in 1838. Other people moved onto the island and the small community of 100 people was wiped out in 1840 by Indians. The key has remained uninhabited since.

NEW SMYRNA (Volusia Co.)
class B-plantation town

Located on SH 44, about two miles west of New Smyrna Beach, this old town dates to 1768, when Andrew Turnbull imported a number of European workers to work his sugar plantation. A small town was established for them, but by the 1770s, they tired of Turnbull's politics, and moved north to nearby St. Augustine.

For the researcher...

BIERA-MAR (Dade Co...destroyed by a 1926 hurricane), GOODNO (Glades Co...cattle town!), KING'S FERRY (Nassau Co...old ferry across the St. Mary's River), LOW TOWN (Charlotte Co...old pirate ghost town), TEMPLE (Bradford Co...south of Lawtey).

Georgia

AURARIA (Lumpkin Co.)
class Db-gold mining

Six miles southwest of Dahlonega.

In 1830, Auraria was one of Georgia's first gold rush towns, booming to a population of 1000. It was also one of the richest and most prosperous towns in the region. When county seat honors were about to be awarded, Auraria put in a bid, but clear ownership of some property couldn't be made, so the honors were awarded to nearby Dahlonega.

This nearly killed the town, but Auraria managed to keep alive, and today is a sleepy backroad burg with 20 people.

DAHLONEGA (Lumpkin Co.)
class E-gold mining

On US 19, 66 miles northeast of Atlanta.

This busy little town of 3000+ is in the heart of Georgia's gold rush country. Its gold deposits were discovered around 1829, and in 1830, the state of Georgia claimed the land, ousting the Cherokee Indians. People flocked to the new found gold fields, but in 1849 after news of the California gold discovery reached the east, many miners headed west, and the workings were nearly deserted, even though the mines continued to produce. They operated through the early 1900s, and resurged somewhat during the Depression, but closed for good in 1942.

The town was considered important enough that in

1833 it became the county seat of newly formed Lumpkin County, and in 1838, the United States government erected a branch mint in Dahlonega to coin some of the locally produced gold (as well as that from Alabama, North Carolina and Virginia). It operated continuously until 1861 and the onset of the Civil War, when the government shut it down. The mint manufactured $1, $2.50, $3, and $5 gold coins.

For a decade the old mint building sat unused, and undamaged by the ravages of the war. In 1871 the North Georgia College converted the building into the state's mining school, but in 1878 it burned.

Dahlonega today is a quiet town that capitalizes on its golden past.

FREDERICA/FORT FREDERICA (Glynn Co.)

class B(NM-$)-military post/settlement

On St. Simons Island, northeast of Brunswick.

The British established Fort Frederica in 1736. After the fort was established, the town of Frederica was established outside the stockade, eventually growing to a population of about 1000.

In 1749 the military presence lessened, which hurt the town's economy. Then in 1758 a fire destroyed most of the town, and finally in 1763 the fort was abandoned.

Today the fort's ruins are a national monument, and various exhibits explain how life was for the British settlers in the early 1700s.

Other ghost towns in Georgia include...

FORT KING GEORGE (McIntosh Co.)

class B/F (restored-$)-British settlement

A mile east of US 17, outside Darien, on a peninsula overlooking the Altamaha River. This was

Britain's southernmost settlement and fort until Ft. Frederica was established. It was established in 1721, and abandoned in 1732. It has been restored.

NEW EBENEZER (Effingham Co.)
class B-German colony

Just off SH 275, 13 miles north of Rincon, this small colony was established by a group of Salzburg Lutherans. In 1736 they relocated six miles to the east, and in 1741 the first church building was built. A grist mill, sawmill and rice mill followed, but in 1779 the British ran them out. A few buildings and a museum remain.

For the researcher...

ABERCORN (Effingham Co...1733-1740), HARDWICKE (Bryan Co... lasted from 1754-early 1800s), LUTHERTOWN (McDuffie Co...an 1880's sawmill town), SAPELO BRIDGE (McIntosh Co...1793-1818), TRAVELER'S REST (Stephans Co...tavern built in 1820).

South Carolina

CHARLESTOWNE LANDING (Charleston Co.)
class C/F (restored-SHP/NR-$)-colonial settlement

On west side of the Ashley River, northwest of downtown Charleston, and part of that city.

In April 1670, a ship full of English colonists landed on Albemarle Point and established a colony. They built a stockade around the site and the colony prospered. In 1680 the settlers crossed to the east side of the river, and what is now Charleston was born. The old site fell into disuse and faded away. In 1970, the state obtained the site and restored it to what it looked like at its peak.

MANCHESTER (Sumter Co.)

class B-cotton shipping center

On SH 261, five miles south of Wedgefield in Manchester State Forest.

In the 1790s, Manchester was a stage stop and way station. As cotton was produced, it became an important shipping center for steamers heading to and from Charleston.

In 1852 it became a busy railroad center, even though the station was a half mile from the town proper. The town was loaded with saloons and horse racing was a popular diversion. During the Civil War it was raided and destroyed by Union troops, but after the war the citizens rebuilt.

The nearby town of Wedgefield was made the railroad's main shipping center in 1872, which killed the economy of Manchester. Within a few years Manchester died. Its site is now marked by a historical marker.

Other ghost towns in South Carolina include...

BRATTONSVILLE (York Co.)

class C/F (restored)-rural community

On Brattonsville Road, off SH 322, five miles east of McConnels. The four buildings that are standing were restored to late 1700s and1800s specifications.

DORCHESTER (Dorchester Co.)

class B (SP)-Colonial settlement

On SH 642, six miles south of Summerville. On east bank of the Ashley River. Founded in 1696 by a group of English Congregationalists from Dorchester, Massachusetts. A fort was established, to protect the colony. In the 1750s, most of the citizens moved to Georgia, and in 1781, the fort and what remained of the town were destroyed by British troops. The foundations have been excavated.

JOHN H. GOODWIN HOUSE (Greenville Co.)
class E (NR)-roadside tavern

Located on US 25, 20 miles north of Greenville, this privately owned landmark is a two story wooden tavern/ inn was originally built around 1790 or so. In 1840 it underwent extensive remodling. In the late 1800s a single story store was added at the site.

For the researcher...

LANDSFORD TOLLHOUSE (Chester Co...canal toll station), SANTA ELENA (Beaufort Co...old Spanish settlement of late 1500s), SIX-MILE HOUSE (Charleston Co... early 1800s tavern, TUNNEL HILL (Oconee Co...once had 1500 people), WINYAH BAY (Georgetown Co...Spanish colony of 1526-1527).

Gary Speck

Dust in the Wind

Epilogue

Glossary of Terms & Abbreviations Used

Abandoned... Generally used for locations or unoccupied structures that have been deserted by their owners, and "left to the elements".

Adit... Horizontal or slightly sloping mine entrance.

BLM...US Dept. of the Interior, Bureau of Land Management.

CCC... Civilian Conservation Corps. A 1930s governmental job program employing people to build roads, trails, or other improvements on government held land.

CR #... County Road/Route number.

Downtown Core...A cluster of commercial buildings making up the business district of a town.

Forest Service...US Dept. of Agriculture, Forest Service.

FR #... Forest Service road.

Ghost Towns...see definition in the Introduction.

There are five major classifications of ghost towns.

A...Site...nothing remains at the location.

B...Rubble/Ruins...No standing buildings, but collapsed walls, foundations, holes, trash dumps, and other debris may remain.

Class B ghost town site.

C...True Ghost...standing unoccupied buildings, no population.

D/a...Near Ghost...see definition below

/b...Semi-Ghost...see definition below.

E...Active small town. Generally it is a historic community that is still busy and active, even if the population is lower than the boom days. Good examples would be Deadwood, SD, Jerome AZ, & Virginia City, NV.

F...Commercial... Not really a classification but an addition to any of the above classes. Generally a restored location, or one that charges a fee to visit.

Ghost Towner...A person who enjoys visiting ghost towns.

Glory Hole...SEE Stope

Government Mine Closing Order (1942)... In 1942 the United States Government required that non-essential businesses close down until WW II ended. This included most gold and silver mines.

Hard Rock Mines/Mining...A method of mining where the miners would dig underground to obtain the ore-bearing rock.

I-#... Interstate highway.

Mining Camp...A small community that grew up around a mine. They were usually established in more remote areas.

Near Ghost Town...A subjective term used usually to denote the fact there are still a few people left in a town that has more abandoned than occupied buildings. More deserted than a "Semi-Ghost Town".

NHD...National Historic District...A historical site of national importance. May or may not be marked by a monument or plaque.

NHL... National Historic Landmark...see NHD

NHP...National Historic Park...see NHD

NHS...National Historic Site...see NHD

NR...National Register...A site of historic importance placed on the National Register of Historic Places.

NRA... National Recreation Area.

Placer Mines/Mining...A method of mining in which the gold is found loose in sand or gravel, and is usually extracted by using water or air movement to separate the heavier gold from the lighter sand and gravel.

Semi-Ghost Town...A subjective category of town where the population has decreased remarkably from the boom days, and the location has many unoccupied or abandoned structures. A little more populated than a "Near Ghost Town" would be.

SH #... State Highway.

Shaft...A vertical entrance or passageway in a mine.

SHL... State Historic Landmark...A protected site registered with the historical commission of a state. It is usually marked with a type of historical marker or plaque.

SHM... State Historic Monument...see SHL and SHP

SHP...State Historic Park...A location of historic importance, sometimes with the buildings being restored to their period appearance.

SHS...State Historic Site...see SHL and SHP above.

SSH #...Secondary State Highway...popular in New Jersey.

Stope...A large room in an underground mine where ore was removed. Often called a glory hole.

Tailing Pile...Piles of dirt and rock left over from mining and milling processes. They are usually located near the mine opening or milling sites.

True Ghost Town...A completely abandoned town with buildings still standing.

Unoccupied...A standing building that is vacant. It may or may not be abandoned.

US #...Federal highway.

$...Entrance fee charged.

Researching Ghost Towns

To be a successful ghost towner, you must learn how to be a successful researcher. The purpose of this section is not teach you how to research (that would be a book in itself!), but give a few pointers that I have found work for me.

GETTING STARTED

Cultivating an insatiable curiosity and an open mind are two of the biggest keys to successful research...that and accurate notetaking. Also, follow-up on all clues. If you do, you will actually end up with more information on more locations than you will ever possibly be able to visit! I KNOW!

LIBRARY

When researching the history of ghost towns, look beyond the obvious books in the local history/travel section. Look for governmental publications, microfilmed copies of old newspapers or maps, and browse the "Readers Guide to Periodical Literature" under "Cities and Towns: Ruined Extinct". Other not so obvious resources include unpublished manuscript collections, and master and doctorate thesis collections. Make friends with the research room librarian!

PERIODICALS

The best periodicals to research for ghost town information are metal detector hobbyist magazines such as Western & Eastern Treasures (has a monthly column on ghost towns by this author) and Lost Treasure; travel and regional magazines such as Desert (out of print), Westways, Southern Living, Lake Superior, and others.

Also check back issues of local newspapers (visit the publisher and go through the "morgue"). Many times papers will publish articles of local interest on little known local ghost towns.

TOURISM AGENCIES

The annual travel guides and official state maps issued by state tourism agencies will often make mention of a site, then you can follow up. Many times they will issue special "guides to historical sites". Also, Automobile clubs such as AAA publish annual tour books, which contain a wealth of useful information.

HISTORICAL SOCIETIES

This is an obvious research key. A well written letter to the society in the state or county of interest will often bring more information than you expect! Just be sure to give them the names and approximate locations of the sites you are interested in, or focus on a small area. They usually can't help much on general "What Ghost Towns are there in your...?"

PRIVATE INDIVIDUALS

In your travels don't be afraid to speak with local inhabitants. Many times you'll find one that's an expert on local history or can refer you to someone who is. I have used this technique many times and it has been immensely valuable. At least a dozen locations in this book are here because an individual told me about the location, and I followed up with research in the county or state historical society.

VERY IMPORTANT

Whenever you send a letter to a private individual, ALWAYS include a Self Addressed Stamped Envelope (SASE) for their reply. It is common courtesy, and many times will make the difference between your letter being answered and thrown away.

Lastly...Don't call 'em ghost towns. Outside of the western United States, most people have a mis-perception that ghost towns are only found in the West. Use terms like "abandoned farming towns", "faded river ports", "the site of that old town on Smith's farm", etc. You will get a lot farther, and maybe have a few more doors open.

Above all, be polite, be professional, and have fun.

The Last Word

Researching and exploring ghost towns has been a popular past-time for many Americans for over a hundred years. The advent of the automobile has made ghost towns much more accessible, both for legitimate visits as well as less legitimate ones. After WW II, a renewed interest in the history and legends of the Old West began, and thousands of weekend adventurers purchased military surplus Willys-Jeeps. These four wheel drive vehicles enabled explorers to reach into extremely remote country and the popularity of ghost towns began.

The interest in ghost towns today has expanded to where people from all walks of life visit these crumbling ghosts of the past. They may be retired 65 year old veterans with 40 years of back country, metal detecting, and four-wheel drive exploration experience, or 25 year old CPAs taking a spouse and infant on their first motorhome cruise through ghost towns along a state highway.

The vast majority of people that visit ghost towns whether just for the thrill of the visit, or for more tangible reasons such as metal detecting or relic hunting, cause no problems. They respect the old buildings for what they are. If they are metal detectorists or relic hunters, they practice "Low Impact Visitation". They do not dig around walls or foundations, and they refill any holes they dig. After they leave, little marks their passage other than footprints.

Even now, relic hunting and treasure hunting in ghost towns is still practiced, but due to local and state ordinances and Federal antiquity laws, the practice is coming under intense scrutiny and control. Right or wrong, as America's ghost towns begin to disappear, there is a strong governmental movement to protect them from the people, even though they belong to the people.

As ghost town lovers we must make our voices heard. It doesn't matter whether you are an avowed metal detectorist, serious historical preservationist, or just a casual visitor, your very right to visit that old ghost town may be in jeopardy if you don't act. Write to your governmental representatives, and voice your opinions. "The squeaky wheel gets the grease!"

Ghost towns are irreplaceable, and every time a building is destroyed or collapses there is one less structure to visit. If you know of, or see anybody that may be accidentally damaging a site, either through lack of knowledge or finesse, stop and explain the consequences of their actions to them.

If you see anybody purposly damaging a site, get a description of them and their vehicle, and jot down any license plate numbers and report them to the local authorities. DO NOT intervene or confront them, as you may endanger yourself. But if you don't act, you are just as guilty as they are!

By making ourselves known as preservationists, and not exploiters, by reporting vandals and educating others of their actions, we can save what remains of America's ghost towns. If we try to work with the government and reverse some of the locking-out legislation that has been enacted, then we are in a win-win situation. If we convince them that we are on their side, then we can regain our freedom to explore, relic hunt, and metal detect in ghost towns, as long as we do it RESPONSIBLY.

Each of us is an ambassador of our interest. It is up to us individually or through groups to abide by any rules or regulations that have been placed on access or detectability of any sites. Whether we agree or disagree with the rule or regulation is irrelevant. If the rule or regulation is unfair, work through the system to change it. If the site is wide open (no prohibitions), still practice responsible, low-impact visitation.

If we all follow these suggestions, then our American ghost towns will remain with us a little longer.

An unknown person once wrote... "The past belongs to the future...but only the present can preserve it."

To that I would like to add my own personal

credo... "Preservation through education."

When you visit a ghost town please abide by the following "Ghost Towner's" code of conduct...

...The "Treasure Hunters Code of Ethics", is printed monthly in Western & Eastern Treasures Magazine, published by People's Publishing Co., Mercer Island, WA. The "Ghost Towner's Code of Ethics" has been modified from that code and is used here with the permission of People's Publishing Company.

"Ghost Towner's Code of Ethics"

I WILL observe all rules and regulations be they local, state, or national.

I WILL camp and make fires only in designated safe locations.

I WILL leave the land and vegetation as it is.

I WILL fill all holes or excavations.

I WILL remove and properly dispose of any trash I find, and will not litter.

I WILL respect the rights and property of landowners,
leave gates as found, and obey all posted signs.

I WILL NOT destroy, damage or deface any buildings or other structures.

I WILL NOT disturb any structures that are locked or appear to be occupied.

I WILL appreciate and protect this nation's ghost towns and the heritage they represent.

I WILL always conduct myself in a manner that is courteous and polite, and show consideration for others.

Dust in the Wind

About the Author

Author - Gary Speck

Gary B. Speck is a third generation native Californian, and lover of history. Ever since the summer of 1968, when as a teenager he toured the Motherlode Country of Central California, the state's ghost towns became his passion. Coupled with a love for treasure hunting and relic collecting, he started researching their history and visiting them on his own as a college student. In 1978 he published his first article in *Treasure* magazine, and followed up two years later in *Western & Eastern Treasures.* In 1983 he began to write seriously, and expanded his interest from just California to nation-wide. In early 1984 began his popular column in Western & Eastern Treasures called "Ghost Town USA". He has published well over 200 articles, on ghost towns for a variety of different magazines, and is one of the very few writers who specialize in this fascinating subject.

His sense of adventure has allowed him the "privilege" of being buzzed by jet fighters in the Mojave Desert, being run off PUBLIC land by gun-totin' old prospectors, and being bit by a rattlesnake. He has found ghost towns in every state he's visited, and knows there is at least one ghost town site within 50 miles of where YOU live!

Notes